The Other Side of Welfare

A Capital Currents Book, a series that examines ideas and issues of concern to contemporary Americans, from education and welfare to international issues—gives readers insight into the topics that affect our world. Other titles include:

The $100,000 Teacher: A Teacher's Solution to America's Declining Public School System by Brian Crosby

Pamela L. Cave

A Capital Currents Book

Capital Books, Inc.
Sterling, Virginia

Capital Books, Inc.
P.O. Box 605
Herndon, Virginia 20172-0605

ISBN 1-892123-84-3 (alk.paper)

Library of Congress Cataloging-in-Publication Data

Cave, Pamela L.
The other side of welfare : real stories from a single mother/ Pamela L. Cave.
p. cm.
Includes index.
ISBN 1-892123-84-3
1. Single mothers—United States. 2. Public welfare—United States. 3. Child support—United States. 4. Single mothers. I. Title.

HQ759.915 .C38 2002
306.85′6—dc21

2002067710

Printed in Canada on acid-free paper that meets the American National Standards Institute Z39-48 Standard

First Edition

10 9 8 7 6 5 4 3 2 1

Dedication

For Phillip, April, Tricia, Megan, and Thomas.

And for all children who are left to grow up one parent short. With hope, for all America's children, that the casual abandonment of children will no longer be tolerated and that all children will grow up with the support and benefit of both parents whenever possible.

Contents

The Other Side of Welfare

by Pam Cave

There's another side of welfare,
You'll likely never see.
I know that because I've been there.
It's not the place to be.

I've also been in your place,
Quietly considering "those" people with disdain.
I've heard the reports of "freeloaders,"
But I never considered their pain.

My husband left our family.
I was expecting at the time.
Although my heart was breaking,
I was filled with fear inside.

When children are depending on you,
You put your pride aside.
They need your love, your time, your world.
Now alone, you must provide.

The courts are long and slow to move.
Civil justice is not swift.
Therefore, you pray, you hope, you cry.
Your lives are simply adrift.

The agency offers some provision.
For that, you are relieved.
But the forms, the waits, the humiliation . . .
Your character may never be retrieved.

Being "on the dole" is not a sweepstakes.
It is not a productive way to live.
The stereotypes, the looks, the stares,
At times, you have no more to give.

But, when children are depending on you,
You put your pride aside.
They need your love, your time, your world.
And alone, you must provide.

In this debate let's put aside,
The old thoughts and ideas reviews.
Let's look at the beginning and remember,
To create a child, it takes two.

When legislating to where we will go,
Let's look at where we have been.
Please, Congressmen, Senators, Mr. President
Demand parental accountability, before you use your pen.

Preface

It was a cold day in September 1990, when a newly made, "single mom" of three, expecting number four, made her way to the courtroom. Before the scheduled hearing time, she had left her three young children—ages three, two, and one—with the Victims' Assistance Network, because the judge, at a prior court hearing, warned her not to bring the children to court again. She waited nervously outside the courtroom and watched for her husband to arrive. Although she had subpoenaed his roommates as witnesses, she did not expect them to come. She knew that her husband had court-appointed counsel, and she planned to represent her own case.

Her husband had left her and the children in May of that year. She went to the family court for help in getting financial support from him, was directed to social services, and subsequently, public assistance. He did not voluntarily provide support for her and the children. Although they had been in court many times regarding their civil case, she and the children continued to receive welfare, not child support. So she decided to file a criminal case for non-support, as provided by the Code of Virginia.

Late one evening, after the three children were asleep, she asked her neighbor to stay with them while she drove to the county magistrate to request the issuance of a criminal arrest warrant for her husband's willful failure to support the family since May 16, 1990. At first, the magistrate told her to go home, go to bed, and call the family court in the morning. This was not what she wanted to hear, and she persisted with the magistrate until he found his copy of the code.

She argued with the magistrate for at least an hour until he agreed to issue the warrant to arrest her husband. It was after one o'clock in the morning when he less than willingly issued the warrant, claiming that he would "hear about this" from the court. She knew that the criminal approach would be more direct, having already been party to more civil continuances than would be considered reasonable. The criminal route, she thought, would be direct and swift and would result in the prompt implementation of child support enforcement measures.

When the case was called, an assistant to the commonwealth's attorney approached the single mom, indicating that she would represent the state in the case. The assistant said that she did not understand why she had been given a "civil family court" case and that she had no knowledge of the criminal statute. She admitted that she only had had two minutes to prepare, and thus, didn't have much hope of winning. The judge, who was familiar with the case, asked why it was being tried as a criminal case, and the disheartened, single mother told him that the civil proceedings took too long. The judge told her that the burden of proof he required for this criminal charge would likely be too high, and that she would probably not be able to meet it, but the trial proceeded anyway. The husband's attorney relentlessly grilled the eight-month-pregnant witness, repeatedly asking, "Why don't you get a job?"

Although the husband had not paid child support since he left, he told the judge he had, on one visit, ordered a take-out pizza and offered to share it with the children. The judge asked the wife to confirm whether or not the offer of pizza had occurred, and when she said it had, he dismissed the charges. The judge justified his decision, stating that he could not find that the husband willfully, and completely, beyond a reasonable doubt, failed to provide for his family. Although he had left his family and had not paid any child support to his pregnant wife and three small children, he *had* provided a pizza . . . he hadn't completely failed to provide for his family.

Upon hearing this decision, the mother gathered her disbelief, her resentment, her hurt, and her anger and determined that she should channel it all toward the reform of the law regarding child support and the willful failure of parents to provide for their children.

Introduction

I have always been an obsessive-compulsive person. I want things to be done right. I want things to work the way they should. I do not like excuses and I do not tolerate disorder well. After almost five years of fighting the effects of anorexia, I met my future husband in an accidental manner. He was the brother of my sister's boyfriend. He had come home from his air base in Germany to pick up his three-year-old son. It was meeting him that changed, and probably saved, my life.

I was married on May 30, 1986. I was twenty-one years old, and I dropped out of college and moved to Germany. I had no idea where my life was going. I had been involved in my eating disorder for so long, that nothing really mattered to me . . . until I met Eric.

I was the oldest of three and was always a good child. The most trouble I ever got into involved being overly zealous with a school project—so much so that I bothered my teacher to the point she called my parents. I used to get straight A's. I was valedictorian of my junior high school class and president of my high school class. I was winter ball princess and the youngest member of the high school dance team. I was president of my church's youth group and outstanding member of my high school pom-pom squad. I was all of these things. Not because I was popular. I was never popular. I just worked very hard.

When Eric saw a picture of me and expressed interest, I experienced something I had never known before. I didn't date in high school. My date for my junior prom was a friend my dad had flown in from Chicago. I didn't socialize, instead I spent my spare time baby-sitting and working variously as a waitress and as a kennel assistant. No one had ever been interested in me as a result of seeing my picture.

Growing up I lived in a secure, safe family unit. We never went without. We always had what we needed. We were not spoiled, but never had to worry about having food to eat or clothes to wear. I gave up my college education to get married. I became the stepmother to a beautiful three-year-old, blond-haired, blue-eyed little boy named Billy. My experience with Billy began my excursion into the world of single parents and abandoned children.

During my fifteen-year marriage, my husband left our family four times. In 1990, he left for seven and a half years. He returned for 18 months, but left again, and has been gone since January 1, 1999. My five children and I have been recipients of public assistance. We have received cash welfare payments, food stamps, medicaid, and housing assistance. I have had my husband arrested numerous times for nonsupport, and have gone to court in some fifty attempts to receive consistent, timely, adequate child support. At the moment, my family receives no child support, and I have no reasonable hope of collecting any in the near future.

In May of 1992, while I was a student in a paralegal studies program at Georgetown University, I wrote to then President George Bush. President Bush responded to my letter with a handwritten note encouraging me to help others. He pledged to fight for improved child support enforcement and wished me success. I took his words to heart. I began to write and to speak in public. And I hung that letter in a prominent place in my home to remind me that my messy situation could be used for a better purpose. Nine years, and three degrees later, President Bush's letter still hangs in my hallway.

I have encountered numerous single moms and dads, during the course of the last eleven years—some rich, some poor, some young, some old. Some are fighters, others victims. Some have been on welfare, some have not. But, all share the same burden of raising a child alone. This book contains a collection of single-parent stories. Some are mine, some, I have simply observed. It is my hope that this book can be used as an educational tool, a source of entertainment, and most importantly, as motivation to others who find themselves in similar circumstances to not give up.

One

Karen Carpenter Was Dead

Karen Carpenter was dead. And I was on my way. At approximately eighty pounds, my physical body and my mind were being ravaged by the disease known as anorexia nervosa, the ailment of the time. Cherry Boone O'Neil's book, *Starving for Attention,* gave me insight on how to manage my eating disorder, but I was so lost in trying to live that I could not focus on a future.

As the oldest of three children, I grew up in a stable family where I never wanted for anything. My brother, sister, and I were the steadfast priorities of both of our parents. My parents always put our needs before their own. Although our lives were not perfect, I had a good home, support for my schoolwork and activities, and parents who were concerned enough to instill rules and discipline.

I never knew what a food stamp was, and I certainly never imagined that parents would so easily and readily leave their children. I was, perhaps, sheltered from some of the realities of life that I would later find myself caught up in. I grew up very well. I wanted to succeed and to please my parents, and I wanted to repay them for all they had given to me.

As a child, I never understood why my birthday was a celebration for me. I thought it should have been a day for me to thank my parents for giving me life, not a day for me to get presents. I was never happy with myself. I felt awkward and out of place as a child. I tried hard to please others and wanted desperately to be liked.

Although I was president of my high school class, a winter ball princess, the only sophomore to make the high school dance team, and the president of my church youth group, I was never popular. I just worked very hard. I had, and continue to have, a mind-set of self-doubt and a belief that I never accomplish enough.

While growing up, I did not have dreams of being a professional person—not a doctor or a lawyer, or even a teacher. I wanted to be a mom. I wanted to find a husband who would provide for our family, be stable, and more, not necessarily a large income, but enough to meet our needs. I wanted to be important to someone without having to work hard at it. I did not date in high school. When I was a winter ball princess, my date, Paul, agreed to accompany me because the word around school was that I liked him. I don't think we said two words to each other all night, and we never went out together again. For my senior prom, my dad flew in my good friend Randy, from Chicago, to be my escort. He wanted me to go to my one and only prom.

After high school, I too-seriously dated a Virginia Military Institute cadet named Karl. We were making plans to get married after he graduated from VMI. I was recovering from my anorexia, and Karl was my entire life. One afternoon, out of the blue, he took me to a park where we frequently walked together, and he told me that because he couldn't lay down his life for me he had to break up with me. I was devastated. After the breakup, I was certain that I would never again, find anyone who would want me. I felt ashamed and worthless.

This mind-set led me to return to my self-destructive anorexic behavior, and in all likelihood led me to marry and have five children with someone who didn't care for or about me.

Life as an anorexic is a hell of its own. Certainly, it is not horrific in the way that war is hell, or in the way that it might be to be born into a third-world, poverty stricken country. But, living with anorexia is living with an ongoing war in your psyche. Everyday when I woke up, I began to worry about what I would, or would not, eat that day. Each day was a struggle. It was not that I thought not eating would bring me happiness. I was just in desperate need, in a desperate search, for some control of my life. I didn't know what or where I wanted to be. I felt like I had no reason for being. Controlling this one area of my life gave me a small sense of purpose.

There were periods of time when I did not eat for two weeks. There were other weeks when I ate nothing solid, but simply drank apple juice. I took diet pills. I took laxatives . . . sometimes more than one hundred a day. I drank syrup of ipecac to make myself throw up when I found I was incapable of forcing myself to vomit on my own. I did all of these things in some twisted, nonsensical effort to gain control. It was a torturous way to live my early college years.

I often wonder what led me to the life I have been living. I never went without the things every child needs growing up. I was not neglected or abused. I was provided every opportunity to become a well-educated and productive adult. But instead of choosing the path leading to an immediate college education, a solid career, and a secure family life, I choose a path that led to welfare.

Throughout my career as an attorney, I have continued to encounter people who find themselves in situations similar to mine. I feel incredibly privileged to have been able to achieve my goal of becoming an attorney and to be able to help others in ways that I wasn't when I was in the same boat. In 1990 and 1992, when I contacted the legal aid agency I now work for, my request for assistance was denied. I was told that my case was too complex and that legal aid resources were limited. As a result of being turned away, today I won't turn my back on someone who has a complex case simply because of the amount of time or resources the case might require. I know that access to legal help in desperate times is too fundamentally important to the well-being of abandoned and deserted families for me to turn them away.

During the year between my first attempt at the Virginia bar exam and my third and final attempt, I was a law clerk for a family law attorney who had almost twenty-five years of experience. Philosophically, we clashed; I wanted to help people, he wanted to make money. Not that I believed he shouldn't make money. After all, that's what working is about. I needed to make money too, but I also needed to help people. By helping deserted children and single parents who had little hope of giving their children a proper home, or decent food, or an opportunity to have the advantages every parent wants for his or her children, I felt I was actually helping myself.

It is difficult to explain why someone chooses to put him- or herself in a detrimental, sometimes perilous, situation. I cannot say with certainty why I made some of the choices I did . . . choices that led me to have five children with a man, who everyone but me saw as incapable of being a serious husband and father.

As a legal aid lawyer, I frequently handle protective order hearings for women who have been victims of domestic violence. It is my job to listen to their stories with an objective ear. Many times, it is clear that a client has placed herself in a dangerous relationship without giving serious thought to the potential personal jeopardy her choice may have put her in. I can see it, but she cannot. Just as I did not—and perhaps still do not completely—see the endless and ongoing pain my choice of relationship has caused, and will continue to cause, for me.

The dynamics of an emotionally and/or physically abusive relationship between a male and a female are complex and often shadowed by secrecy and Oscar-worthy performances on the part of the abusing partner. I use the terms *male* and *female* because many of my clients have been girls who are sixteen, seventeen, and eighteen years of age, with similar-aged boyfriends. They are not *men* and *women,* but they are trapped in abusive relationships just the same.

Abusive relationships evolve in a circular pattern. Police involvement or court intervention are frequently not enough to stop or remedy a relationship saturated in domestic violence. Many police officers respond to radio calls involving domestic situations with a dubious attitude. Sadly, many couples unnecessarily call police in the midst of an argument, file complaints out of anger, and then drop the complaints before an appointed court date. It is unfortunate for true victims of domestic violence that too many citizens use law enforcement and court services as tools of leverage in their relationships. Too many couples "cry wolf," and too many victims are not believed because of those who abuse the process.

Fraudulent claims of violence are asserted frequently during bitter battles over child custody or support. With the technological advances of digital photography, seemingly "real" pictures of false injuries can be offered as evidence in a court proceeding. Innocent women have been convicted of assault as a result of their partner's technological savvy. It is a common phenomena for the abusing partner in a relationship to blame their victim for any and all abuse that may have occurred. Abusive partners displace their blame, deny their involvement, and often attempt to justify their own inappropriate actions.

Court proceedings involving abuse cases are frequently reduced to conflicting testimony of "he said," "she said." A judge cannot make a factual finding that abuse has occurred in a particular situation without adequate, persuasive evidence. It is vitally important that victims of domestic violence immediately report all incidents of abuse, journal and document any violent conduct directed at them by their partner, take clear, actual photographs of injuries sustained as the result of domestic abuse, and seek professional medical treatment. If a victim cannot sufficiently prove domestic violence on the part of their partner, that victim will likely leave a courtroom without legal protection, and will likely be abused again.

Often, a victim of domestic violence will ask that a judge order the abuser into some type of counseling or anger management program. The intent of such programs is logical and provides hope to victims who just want the abuser to "get better." Sadly, participation in such programs is difficult for any court to monitor and frequently fails to remedy the abuse. The best thing any victim can do to resolve a domestic abuse problem is to get away, for good. The reality is that many partners involved in an abusive relationship are compelled to try to "fix" or "change" the other person. Usually such efforts are to no avail.

The majority of victims in abusive relationships are women. Many women who find themselves abused, abandoned, and left to care for small children alone, seek shelter and resources from social service programs. Domestic violence is not limited to the poor. Some women and children in protective shelters have fled from husbands and fathers with six-figure incomes. Domestic abuse and violence frequently leave formerly affluent families no alternative but to seek support from traditional welfare programs. Abusers will just as easily neglect and mistreat their families financially as they will physically.

A classic abuser and irresponsible spouse/parent can be charming, friendly, even likable. Part of the mystique of such a person is the aura he or she creates. Often, outside parties will have no first-hand knowledge of the abuse. Frequently, the abuser is narcissistic and expends great effort trying to convince others that it is the victim who is at fault, the victim who has created the problem. Once this belief has been established, it is difficult to change, and the longer it exists, the more ingrained it becomes in the victim's psyche, and the less likely it is that he or she will have the courage to get away.

As I work with women and men in destructive, domestic circumstances, I must be objective. When I look back on my own circumstance, any objectivity that I might have been capable of achieving was obviously thrown out the window. I have no reasonable explanation for why I stayed and had five children with my husband. We did not plan to have five children together. However, when I married my husband, I took my vows seriously. I meant every word I said. I meant it to be "forever." I have since lived a harsh reality created and embraced by our contemporary American culture. Along with disposable diapers, disposable contact lenses, disposable dishes, and silverware, we also have disposal families. Disposal families are at the heart of America's need for "welfare" and its reform.

Two

A Right without a Remedy

In 1975, the United States Congress passed legislation to create a federal program for child support enforcement. This legislation was created and implemented under Title IV-D of the Social Security Act. The intent behind the original legislation was to facilitate "cost recovery", or in other words, to recoup funds paid out to families with children receiving Aid to Families with Dependent Children, the original "welfare."

In 1996, the United States Congress passed legislation to reform welfare, by abolishing Aid to Families with Dependent Children. The intent behind the 1996 legislation was to facilitate family self-sufficiency by moving families, via specific timeline requirements, from "welfare" to "work." In 1996, Congress failed to sufficiently address the undeniable fact that without adequate, appropriate child support, no single parent family living on minimal income will ever become self-sufficient. Without adequate, appropriate child support, such families will indefinitely require some type of government assistance to survive. My family is a case in point.

Statutes, on their faces, do appear to protect children's rights to child support. The Personal Responsibility and Work Opportunity Reconciliation Act of 1996[1] (PRWORA) requires that states implement specific policies and procedures to improve child support enforcement. The implementation of requirements and their subsequent results are to be reported by states within timelines provided by the act. States must achieve goals in several areas to be eligible for certain types of federal funding and/or federal matching funds. For example, the Commonwealth of Virginia, by statute,[2] requires that parents provide appropriate support for their children. "A child living at home with both parents is entitled to have his basic needs provided. Where a child is separated from one of his parents, the law of this Commonwealth allows the courts to provide for the child's basic needs and, within reason, some measure of assumed parental generosity" (*Conway v. Conway,* 395 S.E. 2d 464, 467 [Va. 1990]).

The federal government spends approximately two billion dollars per year on child support enforcement.[3] Although large sums of government money are spent on the effort, states are failing to collect child support at an acceptable rate. Under federal program requirements, states are collectively failing to collect child support at a rate of 85 percent.[4] This large failure rate precipitated the welfare crisis observed by Congress and the general public. The great burden on the federal government to provide funds for public assistance has been, as determined by some experts, the direct result of states failing to collect child support for the most needy children.[5]

The Federal Rules of Civil Procedure and well-established principles of constitutional law, have together created a domestic relations exception to federal diversity jurisdiction in family law matters. To state this more simply, the federal courts generally do not hear cases involving issues of family law such as child custody, child support, and the like. Individual state courts are the proper courts for the majority of family law disputes. However, the federal government has implemented several uniform acts to further the cause of effective child support across the nation. Experts have counseled federal officials that a comprehensive approach is needed to better child support collections through better child support enforcement.[6]

The structure and composition of the American family, under the influence of a popular, individual-rights-centered culture, has suffered substantial breakdown. This breakdown, as observed over the last thirty years, has led to a predictable, but economically devastating result.[7] Because some parents are not providing adequately, or in some cases at all, for their children, millions of American children are being subjected to a childhood of poverty[8] and a future of uncertainty.

In an initial effort to increase and improve child support enforcement, Congress passed an amendment to the Social Security Act[9] in 1975.[10] The legislative intent of Congress was to establish the child support enforcement system as a joint federal and state effort partially funded by the federal government.[11] This original legislation has been modified and expanded through various subsequent amendments and acts. The Child Support Amendments of 1984[12] created a joint system for child support establishment and enforcement. The federal government directed states to provide child support services to all custodial parents receiving public and/or medical assistance. It then expanded this directive to include the provision of services to any custodial parent who requests child support services.[13]

The Family Support Act of 1988[14] went further than the amendments of 1984 by requiring additional mandates to be placed on the states. The mandates include specific standards for paternity establishment, procedures for income withholding from a noncustodial parent's wages, presumptive guidelines for setting child support awards and orders, requirements for regular, periodic review and adjustment of child support orders, the establishment of statewide automated data systems, and requirements for the reporting of results. Recent estimates indicate that 60 percent of all child support cases are managed within the purview of the IV-D system.[15]

There have been some successes pursuant to federal efforts.[16] However, it is clear that there is a long way to go.[17] The United States Census Bureau published data indicating that in 1991, of the 11.5 million custodial parents entitled to child support for their minor children, 46 percent had no established child support award, 11 percent had an award but received no child support, and, only 24 percent of entitled families with child support awards receive the full amount ordered by a court.[18]

The child support establishment and enforcement reforms mandated by the enactment of the Personal Responsibility and Work Opportunity Reconciliation Act of 1996, have led to numerical improvements with regard to child support collection figures.[19] During the hearing, it was reported that subsequent to 1996, states have begun to utilize additional child support enforcement and collection tools. These tools include the creation of new-hire databases, improved methods of efficient paternity establishment, improved access to and use of financial institution data matches, the revocation of state-issued driver's licenses, and the revocation of other government-afforded privileges for parents delinquent in paying child support.[20]

Data collected and presented regarding the failure of child support enforcement efforts generally seems to indicate that there will never be a perfect child support system. Obviously, the collection system will never collect every dollar. However, there is clearly a large gap between funds that are actually collected and funds that, theoretically, could be collected.[21]

With the enactment of the 1996 welfare reform legislation, the federal Child Support Enforcement program altered its focus from cost-recovery of funds expended through public assistance programs, to fostering family responsibility and promoting family self-sufficiency.[22] In theory, the intent of the legislation is well founded and logically constructed. In 1975, the goal of child support legislation was to recoup welfare money paid out to children by the federal government. States were to track down the absent parent involved and put in place an order, administrative or judicial, requiring that the noncustodial parent "pay back" the welfare money. All of it . . . eventually.

Under the 1975 law, states were provided with great flexibility in the methods used to establish, collect, and enforce child support orders. The flexibility granted to states prior to 1996 contributed to the fact that states were failing to collect child support at a rate of 85 percent.[23] During the national and legislative debate leading up to the enactment of 1996 welfare reform laws, child support reform proposals were offered and considered by federal officials, politicians, child support agency directors, administrators, staff, advocates, members of the bar, and others in the child support enforcement community.[24]

An example of the formidable task of enforcing child support orders is exemplified by a statement made by Mr. Clarence Carter, director of Social Services for the Commonwealth of Virginia. During a state gathering of social workers, advocates, and advisory board members that the state has reached a figure of over 1.2 billion dollars as the amount of past-due child support, on record, and outstanding. He went further and stated that the department holds little hope of ever recovering the money.[25]

The statement made by Mr. Carter represents the fundamental problem. There are too many children who deserve, and are lawfully entitled to, their child support, but, unfairly and tragically will never receive it. There are children in our country, in every state, in every county, who, at no fault of their own, hold little hope of ever receiving the child support they need, they deserve, and they are entitled to. For these children, their right to receive child support will likely remain nothing more than a right without a remedy.

The successful, timely establishment of paternity is key in forming the foundation of effective child support enforcement. Nonpaternity is a common defense presented by potential child support obligors.[26] The State of Washington achieved improved child support collection rates by improving its rate of voluntary paternity establishment.[27] In Massachusetts, a report from April 1994 indicated that in-hospital paternity establishment programs resulted in a 54-percent rate of paternity establishment.[28] Fortunately, there seems to be an increasing change in social perspective regarding the importance of paternity establishment. Establishing paternity opens the door to the receipt of child support. A legal presumption of paternity exists for men whose wives become mothers. Proper paternity establishment in cases where mothers are not married to the fathers of their babies is essential to facilitate a child support order or the subsequent enforcement of that order.

Paternity establishment serves as a springboard to securing an emotional and financial connection between the father and the child. Without such a connection, the child may be denied a lifetime of economic, psychological, and economic benefits. Not only does a legal, parental link open the doors to possible governmental benefits and medical support, it also provides the opportunity for a child to receive less quantifiable benefits, such as the value of knowing his or her biological father, extended family, medical history, and genetic information.[29]

It is vitally important that new mothers protect the rights of their children to receive the support and benefit of their fathers by establishing the paternity of their babies as soon as possible following birth. Mothers should be educated in the hospital regarding the value and importance of legally naming the fathers of their babies. The immediate lawful establishment of paternity will facilitate better child support enforcement and protect any interests in a father's future social security or other legal benefits, which can be directed toward his minor children.

Nationwide, the number of paternities established or acknowledged reached a record 1.6 million in fiscal year 2000.[30] The 1.6 million figure represents an increase of 46 percent since fiscal year 1996. Of the 1.6 million paternities established, more than 688,000 were established through in-hospital acknowledgement programs. An additional 867,000 paternities were established through the federal Child Support Enforcement Program.

From a social and public policy perspective, it is hoped that paternity establishment will engage fathers in the lives of their children, create emotional bonds between fathers and their children, foster a sense of security in children, and help contribute to the needs children have that are crucial to their health and well being. Unfortunately, hoping does not cause fathers to be engaged with their children. Sadly, many dads in the United States do not care if they have a bond with one, or any, of their children.

The Personal Responsibility and Work Opportunity Reconciliation Act of 1996 was crafted with the legislative intent of making the paternity establishment process easier and faster. The act expanded the voluntary in-hospital paternity establishment process begun in 1993 and further, required a state affidavit for voluntary paternity acknowledgment. States must also publicize the availability of the process and must encourage fathers to avail themselves of it.[31]

The ability to locate an absent parent to bring that parent into the child support process is vital to the viability of a potential case. Without the absent parent, proper notice, and the opportunity to contest, the process of seeking and obtaining child support cannot lawfully proceed. Generally, there exists a three-year window in which a missing person can successfully be found based upon known information such as:

1. the last known address,
2. the last known employer,
3. social security number,

4. driver's license information, and
5. a personal credit report.[32]

The federal government has methods available to assist in the process of locating a missing noncustodial parent. The Federal Parent Locator Service (FPLS) can access data from the Internal Revenue Service, the Selective Service System, the Department of Defense, the Social Security Administration, the Veterans' Administration, State Employment Security Agencies, and the National Personnel Records Center.[33] All states could improve efficiency in locating absent parents by tapping into the Federal Parent Locator Service. Unfortunately too many states do not access the variety of federal child support enforcement resources available. As a result, too many children go without the support they deserve to meet their most basic needs.

The national rate of child support collection and enforcement is 37 percent.[34] In excess of $83 billion in child support is outstanding and overdue to 30 million-plus children in the United States today. Approximately 78 percent of noncustodial parents have health insurance. Only 23 percent of those parents extend and make that insurance available to their children. Of families led by single women, never married to the fathers of their children, only 24 percent receive consistent child support payments. And, of families led by single women, divorced from the fathers of their children, only 54 percent receive consistent payments.[35]

Children are entitled to be supported by their parents. Children do not enter the world with the capacity to feed, or clothe, or care for themselves. Although children grow and, eventually, learn to manage these tasks themselves, no child is capable of supporting him or herself from birth through childhood until adulthood.

Too often in our country of prosperity and affluence, parents make children and walk away from those children without ever looking back to provide the food, the clothing, and the care their children require. These adults will proffer lists of weak excuses as to why they cannot support their children . . . after all, they have car payments to make, new adult relationships to sponsor, addictive habits to fund, and selfish desires to satisfy. With all the distractions and enticements of American life, who should expect irresponsible parents to do the right thing? They have not done the "right thing" for years. Without a significant change in social and public, tolerance, regarding parents who abandon their children and families, child support will always be nothing more than a right without a remedy for the majority of our nation's poorest children.

NOTES

1. Pub Law No. 104-193, 110 Stat. 2105 (1996). This act was the final result of a well-publicized and long-fought effort by Congress to reform the welfare system. The act implements time limits for receipt of assistance, work requirements, new eligibility standards for food stamps, a bar to assistance for most legal immigrants, an elimination of a childcare entitlement, and specific limitations for the receipt of assistance by unwed mothers, teenage mothers, and mothers having new children while receiving public assistance. Although, traditionally, issues of family law and domestic disputes have been considered state matters, the Personal Responsibility and Work Opportunity Reconciliation Act (PRWORA) has required states to make significant changes in the area of child support policies and procedures.

2. Virginia Code Section 20-61. (1977). This statute prohibits the desertion and/or nonsupport of children by their parents. "Desertion or nonsupport of wife, husband or children in necessitous circumstances.—Any spouse who, without cause, deserts or willfully neglects or refuses or fails to provide for the support and maintenance of his or her spouse, and any parent who deserts or willfully neglects or refuses or fails to provide for the support and maintenance of his or her child under the age of eighteen years of age, or child of whatever age who is crippled or otherwise incapacitated from earning a living, the spouse, child, or children then being in necessitous circumstances, shall be guilty of a misdemeanor."

3. *Contract with America—Welfare Reform: Hearings before the Subcommittee on Human Resources,* the United States House of Representatives Committee on Ways and Means, the 104th Congress, the First Session (1995), (testimony of Ronald K. Henry of the Men's Health Network, page 1289). Mr. Henry concluded that federal policies regarding parental accountability, "allow children to be held as hostages." Although, he does affirm the fact that under the law of each state, parents have an obligation of financial responsibility for their minor children.

4. *Contract with America—Welfare Reform: Hearings before the Subcommittee on Human Resources,* the United States House of Representatives Committee on Ways and Means, the 104th Congress, the First Session (1995), (testimony of Kevin Aslanian of the National Welfare Reform and Rights Union, page 1350).

5. *Contract with America—Welfare Reform: Hearings before the Subcommittee on Human Resources,* the United States House of Representatives Committee on Ways and Means, the 104th Congress, the First Session (1995), (testimony of Kevin Aslanian of the National Welfare Reform and Rights Union, page 1346).

6. Paul K. Legler, "The Coming Revolution in Child Support Policy: Implications of the 1996 Welfare Act," 30 *Family Law Quarterly* (1996) at 521. See also David T. Ellwood, *Poor Support: Poverty in the American Family* (1988); The United States Bureau of the Census, *Family Disruption and Economic Hardship: The Short-Run Picture for Children* (Current Population Reports Series P-70, No. 23, 1991); and, Mary Jo Bane and David T. Ellwood, "One-fifth of the Nation's Children: Why Are They Poor?" 245 *Science* 1047 (1989).

7. See Working Group on Welfare Reform, Family Support, and Independence, The United States Department of Health and Human Services, *Background Papers on Welfare Reform: Child Support Enforcement* 3 (1994), and *Report to Congress on Out-of-Wedlock Childbearing* (1995); David T. Ellwood and Mary Jo Bane, *The Impact of Aid to Families with Dependent Children on Family Structure and Living Arrangements* (1985).

8. Paul K. Legler, "The Coming Revolution in Child Support Policy: Implications of the 1996 Welfare Act," 30 *Family Law Quarterly* (1996) at 521. The low-income status of female-headed families is often a result of failed policies regarding child support. In 1992, the average income for single mothers with children was $14,517 per year.

9. See Social Security Act of 1935, Public Law No. 74-271, Stat. 620 (codified as amended at 42 United States Code, Sections 601–617, 1935).

10. Public Law No. 93-647, 88 Stat. 2337 (1974). The amendment implemented the requirement that states establish and maintain child support enforcement programs. These programs were designated as "IV-D" programs because of the amendment's location in the actual text of the Social Security Act. "Cooperative federalism" requires that states choosing to participate in public assistance programs for dependent children must comply with Title IV-D. States also must comply with IV-D regulations to be eligible for federal funding.

11. Generally, the federal government pays approximately 66 percent of administrative expenditures related to child support enforcement. Incentives equal to 16 percent are also provided by the federal government. See The United States House of Representatives Committee on Ways and Means, *Overview of Entitlement Programs,* Table H-27, at 1210 (1994).

12. Public Law No. 93-378, 98 Stat. 1305 (1984). These amendments provided specific directives to the states and mandated the adoption of certain state laws and policies regarding child support enforcement. Pursuant to the directives, states are now required to provide assistance in child support establishment and enforcement on behalf of any child, not only children receiving public and/or medical assistance.

13. See *Carter v. Morrow,* 562 F. Supp. 311 (1983).

14. Public Law No. 100-485, 102 Stat. 2343 (1988).

15. The purview of federal legislation increased with the passing of the Omnibus Budget reconciliation Act of 1993. Public Law No. 103-66, 107 Stat. 312 (1993). This act required states to establish in-hospital paternity determination policies.

16. The annual rate of receipt of child support for women of varied marital status has improved since 1975. For married women, the rate of receipt has increased 92 percent. For divorced women, the rate of receipt has increased 43 percent. For separated women, the rate of receipt has increased 94 percent. And, for never married women, the rate of receipt has increased 250 percent. Total IV-D collections have risen from $3.9 billion, in 1987, to $10.8 billion, in 1995. The number of paternities established has more than doubled since 1987. Finally, child support enforcement, when successful, appears to be cost effective, as nearly four dollars are collected for every dollar spent on the program. See the United States Census Bureau, 1975, *Survey of Income and Education;* and, the 1983 and 1989 Current Population Survey, *Child Support and Alimony Supplement.*

17. Statistics presented by a 1994 study performed by the Urban Institute indicate a large gap between the dollar amount of child support actually collected and the amount that theoretically could be collected. See Elaine Sorenson, The Urban Institute, *Noncustodial Fathers: Can They Afford to Pay More Child Support?* (1994).

18. See the United States Census Bureau, *Child Support for Custodial Mothers and Fathers* (Current Population Reports Series P60-187, 1991).

19. Remarks included in the opening statement of Chairman Wally Herger, The Subcommittee on Human Resources, The United States

House of Representatives Committee on Ways and Means; *Hearing on Child Support and Fatherhood Proposals,* Thursday, June 28, 2001.

20. Statement of Chairman Wally Herger, The Subcommittee on Human Resources, The United States House of Representatives Committee on Ways and Means, *Hearing on Child Support and Fatherhood Proposals,* Thursday, June 28, 2001. "This Subcommittee has and will continue to monitor the effects of such changes. Here is what we know already. In 2000, $17.9 billion in child support was collected, which is a 50 percent increase since 1996. By using the passport denial program, $7 million in lump-sum payments were collected in the last year, and the number of paternities established in 2000 reached a record 1.6 million, an increase of 46 percent since 1996. Overall, the system seems to be operating more efficiently with total collections per program dollars spent on the rise as well. Yet, with all that, we also know that in 1999, the program collected child support payments for only 37 percent of its caseload."

21. According to a 1994 study by Elaine Sorenson of the Urban Institute, the uncollected amount of child support due to children each year is in excess of $33.8 billion. Of that figure, 21 percent is not collected due to the failure to collect what is ordered, another 21 percent is not collected due to the inadequacy of child support awards, and 58 percent is not collected due to the fact that many custodial parents simply do not have a legal child support award or order. The amount of child support that was received during the study was $14.4 billion. If child support orders had been fully enforced, cumulative child support payments should have been in excess of $48.2 billion. (The study reflected figures from 1990). Elaine Sorenson, the Urban Institute, *Noncustodial Fathers: Can They Afford to Pay More Child Support?* (1994).

22. Statement of Frank Fuentes, acting deputy commissioner, the Office of Child Support Enforcement Administration for Children and Families, United States Department of Health and Human Services. Statement submitted for the record: The Subcommittee on Human Resources, The United States House of Representatives Committee on Ways and Means, *Hearing on Child Support and Fatherhood Proposals,* Thursday, June 28, 2001.

23. According to the National Welfare Rights and Reform Union, children and families were not receiving the child support they were entitled to due to "irresponsible behavior" on the part of the child support bureaucracy. The organization asked Congress, "What kind of legislative proposals are there to address the irresponsible behavior

of child support bureaucrats?" *Contract with America: Hearings before the Subcommittee on Human Resources,* The United States House of Representatives Committee on Ways and Means, 104th Congress, First Session (1995), (testimony of Kevin Aslanian). Page 1346.

24. In June of 1993, President Bill Clinton appointed a "working group" to address welfare reform with an emphasis on child support enforcement. A subgroup, entitled the "Child Support Issue Group," did a majority of policy proposals and development for the final legislation submitted by the president. Members of the working group included representatives of the Federal Office of Child Support Enforcement, the National Child Support Enforcement Association, the Administration for Children, Youth, and Families, the United States Department of Health and Human Services, the National Women's Law Center, the American Bar Association, the American Public Welfare Association, the Women's Legal Defense Fund, the Children's Defense Fund, the Center for Law and Social Policy, and the Office of Assistant Secretary for Planning and Evaluation. The expertise of many was considered in the development of recent federal child support legislation. However, the results of success thus far are disappointing. The Working Group on Welfare Reform, Family Support, and Independence, the United States Department of Health and Human Services, *Background Papers on Welfare Reform: Child Support Enforcement* 3, (1994). The opinions expressed by the members of the working group pressed for better, tighter policies regarding child support enforcement not only because it would, conceivably, save tax dollars. (It would dollar-for-dollar reduce welfare expenditures.) The general opinions expressed claimed in unison that children have a fundamental right to child support from their parents. It would seem that this expression would lead to the conclusion that a constitutional claim might be made. However, the need for better child support enforcement was narrowed to the following statement: "It's the right thing to do." *Child Support Enforcement and Welfare Reform: Hearings before the United States House of Representatives Committee on Ways and Means Subcommittee on Human Resources,* 104th Congress, First Session (1995), (testimony of David Ellwood).

25. These facts were reported to the Fairfax County Advisory Social Services Board by Department of Family Services' staff member, Kathy Froyd. She had been delegated by the department as its representative to a meeting held in Southern Virginia on November 20, 1997. The reporting of the event occurred at an Advisory Social Services Board meeting held December 2, 1997.

26. Any absent father brought into an administrative proceeding or before a court may claim nonpaternity as a defense to having a child support obligation. For a variety of reasons, a man may claim that he is not the father of the child or children concerned. Most courts find that a mother and father are implicitly bound by the implication of paternity that exists in a divorce or support proceeding. Some courts may allow a non-paternity claim subsequent to divorce if the issue was not raised during the divorce proceeding. In cases where paternity is truly in question, the facts may require the collection of evidence to determine paternity to facilitate the process of establishing a child support order. Without the establishment of paternity one way or another, there can effectively be no legally binding obligation. *Effective Enforcement Techniques for Child Support Obligations,* 2nd Edition. The United States Department of Health and Human Services, Office of Child Support Enforcement, and the National Institute for Child Support Enforcement. Barbara Roberts, J.D., Michael R. Henry, J.D., and, Lavon Loynd, J.D. (1987).

27. The State of Washington implemented an innovative program to obtain the voluntary establishment of paternity in hospitals at the time of a child's birth. The program provided an immediate opportunity, following birth, for parents to sign affidavits establishing parentage. The success realized by this effort led to the inclusion of a similar provision by the Clinton Administration in the Omnibus Budget Reconciliation Act of 1993. Generally, an affirmative declaration of paternity is essential to pursue the establishment of a formal child support order. Washington experienced a 37-percent rate of paternity establishment via the program. Washington State Office of Child Support Enforcement, Paternity Acknowledgement Program: Program Summary (1991).

28. The report concluded that in 54 percent of births to unmarried mothers, fathers had voluntarily acknowledged paternity in the hospital. An additional 10 percent did so later at the offices of town officials or clerks. In Massachusetts, the Department of Revenue requires the father of a child to affirmatively acknowledge paternity before his name can appear on the child's birth certificate. Marilyn Ray Smith, chief legal counsel, child Support Enforcement Division for the Massachusetts Department of Revenue. *Policy Studies, Inc., Massachusetts Paternity Acknowledgement Program: Implementation, Analysis, and Program Results.* (1995).

29. An extended discussion of the need for and benefits of efficient paternity establishment is presented in the *Background Papers on Welfare Reform.* Paul K. Legler, attorney advisor to the assistant secretary

for Planning and Evaluation, the United States Department of Health and Human Services, elaborates on the paternity issue in "The Coming Revolution in Child Support Policy: Implications of the 1996 Welfare Act."

30. Statement of Frank Fuentes, acting deputy commissioner, Office of Child Support Enforcement Administration for Children and Families, the United States Department of Health and Human Services, Thursday, March 15, 2001. The United States House of Representatives Ways and Means Committee, Subcommittee on Human Resources.

31. Statement of Frank Fuentes, acting deputy commissioner, the Office of Child Support Enforcement Administration for Children and Families, the United States Department of Health and Human Services, Thursday, March 15, 2001. The United States House of Representatives Ways and Means Committee, Subcommittee on Human Resources.

32. As a general rule, private investigators, private agencies, and companies designed to locate missing persons advertise that they can locate any missing person, provided that person has had some personal information available within the three years prior to the start of the search. These advertisements appear in the advertising section of the *American Bar Association Journal* on a regular basis.

33. The FPLS can provide social security numbers, addresses, employer and wage information, and information regarding employment compensation.

34. Statement of Nathaniel L. Young Jr., director, the Virginia Department of Social Services' Division of Child Support Enforcement, Richmond, Virginia; president, National Council of Child Support Directors; board member, National Child Support Enforcement Association; and board member, Eastern Regional Interstate Child Support Association, Thursday, March 15, 2001. The United States House of Representatives Ways and Means Committee, Subcommittee on Human Resources.

35. Statistics reported by the Association for Children for Enforcement of Support, Inc., Spring 2002, *Aces National News*. (926 J St., Suite 1216, Sacramento, California, 95814, 1-800-738-2237, www.childsupport-ACES.org).

Three

A Teenage Mom

Kelly was fifteen years old when she discovered she was pregnant. Teenage pregnancy was not new to her family. Her older sister had become pregnant in high school, too. Her sister had married, had several children, and eventually, but not too long thereafter, divorced. Kelly was not ready to lead the life her sister had led. Out of fear and desperation, she took diet pills in an attempt to abort the baby. Kelly was my husband's first wife. She was married as a high school sophomore, instantly becoming both military wife and mother. I learned about Kelly and the struggles she had gone through as I cleaned out a storage closet in a high-rise building known as the "China Wall" in a small German town called Nieder Roden. As I looked through her wedding album and the first few completed pages of her newborn son's, baby book, I gleaned an unknowing glimpse of the future before me.

I didn't quite understand the story from the start. Eric, my then new husband, had been married at the age of nineteen, to Kelly, then fifteen. Together, they had had Billy, a baby boy who was effectively deserted at the tender age of three by his young mother. As I read through her wedding album and prebaby notes, it became sadly clear that although Kelly had been physically mature enough to have a baby, she was nowhere close to being emotionally mature enough. She was a smitten school girl. Her notes were laced with romantic notions of married life and motherhood. Her photo albums depicted what could have been a happy family of three. Instead, reality was that the family of three consisted of a teenager not ready to be a mother, an enlisted airman not ready to be a father, and a baby, needing but lacking both.

The couple married in the fall of 1982. Their baby was born in February 1983. As many young, enlisted military couples do, they struggled. With little money, no experience, and too much unwanted responsibility, Eric and Kelly attempted to make their marriage, and their family, work. Unfortunately, it was a union doomed to fail. The couple, briefly, shared a home at a military base in Georgia. As an enlisted airman working in the commissary, Eric spent long hours away from home. As a teenager, just sixteen, Kelly was left alone for most of every day, to be a mother. Because she had never finished high school, Kelly studied to earn a GED. I remember reading notes in which Kelly tried to rationalize that a GED would be just as good as a high school diploma. The notes were disturbing because the text expressed a longing not for the credential itself, but for the experience of finishing high school. She was a baby, raising a baby, and she had a husband whose maturity level was questionable, at best. Kelly went home to her mother, repeatedly, to seek help with the baby and to seek help for herself.

When Billy was just eighteen months old, he reached up to a stove and tipped a pot of boiling water over on himself, scalding his skin. The young parents rushed to the hospital to treat the burn. Although Billy's skin would eventually heal, the recovery process was painful. Kelly, being a young, inexperienced mother, had difficulty changing the bandages, dealing with the extent of the burn and its resulting wilted skin, and learning to have patience to care for her injured baby. Kelly went home to her mother, again.

Soon after the burn occurred, Eric took an assignment at Rhein-Main Air Force Base in Germany. He hoped that moving his young family away from Virginia and completely out on their own would keep Kelly home, and would give them a chance to make their marriage work. But things were worse in Germany. Eric's hours increased, and Kelly felt increasingly isolated. Not only did Eric work at the base commissary, he also began to work at the base troop support station. He would leave at 5:00 A.M. and return after 7:00 P.M. The days were long for Kelly, and for Billy.

When Eric returned home, he ate and went to sleep on the couch. There was no respite for the young mother. No time for herself. No help with Billy. No chance to socialize with people her own age. She was in a foreign country with no friends, no help with her baby, and too much responsibility. Kelly began to seek out friends her own age.

She began to leave Billy at home at night with a father who fell asleep with little regard for the consequences of leaving a two-year-old child unattended. Billy spent hours in his crib, wearing the same clothing all day long. When the baby cried incessantly, his parents put his crib in a large closet so that his cries would not be heard by passersby in the apartment hallway.

The tension that grew in that tiny apartment eventually boiled over. Eric and Kelly had a physical altercation where she kicked him and he pinned her against the wall. Soon afterward, Eric came home from work to an empty apartment. Kelly had, once again, gone home to her mother, for the last time.

I first met Eric and Billy during the winter of 1985. Eric, an enlisted airman still stationed in Rhein-Main, Germany, had returned to the states that Christmas for two reasons. One, to finalize his divorce from Kelly, and two, to get Billy. Eric was not prepared to be a single parent. He could hardly take care of himself. Billy and I would learn that the hard way.

I was an undecided, unmotivated undergraduate student at Virginia Tech in Blacksburg, Virginia. Although I had gained weight and no longer looked like an anorexic, my mind-set continued to be that of an anorexic. Socially, I just didn't seem to fit in. I had been involved in an intense and overly serious relationship with a cadet from Virginia Military Institute during my recovery. It had been my first relationship, and it ended suddenly. I was devastated.

During my first quarter at Virginia Tech, I struggled academically. My concentration was poor, and every class was difficult. Before I developed anorexia, I was a top student. After anorexia, I was average, at best. I had no goals, no motivation. I did not know what I wanted to do with my life, or where I wanted to do it. My sister and brother were also students at Virginia Tech. They were both doing well academically and were both successful socially. I was the odd one out. I knew that, and I kept to myself.

On Christmas night 1985, I drove my sister to Winchester, Virginia, to visit her boyfriend, because my dad didn't want her to drive there alone. It was about a ninety minute drive. My sister's boyfriend was generally not forthcoming with information about his family. Although he mentioned bits and pieces, he seemed to be embarrassed by them and never went into detail.

One of the embarrassments was his brother, Eric. Eric had been married right out of high school, had a baby, enlisted in the military, and was home from Germany to get divorced and take custody of his three-year-old little boy. Kelly, the baby's mother, had decided she just couldn't handle him anymore and left him with his father to fly on an airplane, across the ocean, to a life of little attention, little supervision, and little, if any, discipline. The scenario included all the components needed for a tragic soap opera. Unfortunately, it was not a soap opera. It was, four months later, to become my life.

When I met Eric, he looked too much like an overgrown teenager. Wearing a rock concert T-shirt and sporting a military haircut, there was an obvious dichotomy about him. He smoked, which I hated. His teeth were stained from the combination of cigarette smoke and a steady diet of coffee, but, I was instantly attracted to him. When Eric was clean, he was strikingly handsome. No one like him had ever been interested in me. From the moment I met him, I was inextricably attached. To this day, I don't know why. His life was a mess. He had a three-year-old boy to care for and no clue how to do it. He was obviously very needy . . . and, I guess, so was I.

We spent most of the few days he spent stateside talking on the telephone, going to a movie, and spending time together. Eric had finished high school, but he was not academically inclined to do more. Eric was a talented football player and a good athlete. Although he had only average high school grades, he had been offered remote opportunities to play football for Southern Methodist University and Shippensburg University. Unfortunately, his choice to engage in an adult relationship with Kelly meant that his football dreams would be tossed away . . . forever.

Our time together was short, but intense. We had nothing in common. I had always been good. He seemed to have always been bad. I was voted "most shy" in my senior class. He was voted "biggest flirt." No two people could have been more poorly suited for each other. Eric had more problems than I could fathom. He was just recently divorced, and he had to return to a foreign country with a little boy who hardly knew him. As an enlisted E-4 in the United States Air Force, his income was approximately $13,000 per year. He worked in the Air Force Commissary Service and did not appear to have much motivation to improve his financial situation, his educational background, or his broken family relationships. On top of all that, he smoked. He still does. I hate smoking, but I was willing to tolerate it. From the first time we met, I knew that I desperately loved him, for some unknown reason. From that first moment on Christmas Day 1985, I was sure that my life would be inextricably intertwined with his . . . forever.

I watched Eric and Billy board their flight for Germany several days before New Year's Eve. As he left, he told me that we would keep in touch, but I knew that with a huge ocean between us, all of the keeping in touch would be confined to my telephone calls, cards, and letters. The cost of postage and phone calls would be prohibitive, considering the money I had available to me. Although I baby-sat for a university professor, my monthly income was pretty much limited to the money my parents gave me for living expense's, which was sufficient for my life at Virginia Tech, but wasn't enough to support the long-distance relationship I contemplated.

Several weeks after classes resumed, I was awakened by the ringing of a telephone at 5:45 A.M. Half asleep, I answered and heard Eric on the other end. "Hey, what are you doing?" he asked. To this day, he answers the phone the same way. I was very surprised to hear from him. We pretty much small-talked for about an hour. He did indicate, however, that he was having trouble adjusting to having Billy with him full time. It was difficult to be a single dad in the military. His hours were strict, his schedule, tight, and there was not much room for flexibility. Being only three years old, newly abandoned by his young mother, and living in a strange country where nothing was familiar, Billy, too, was having trouble adjusting to being with Eric full time. They were virtually strangers who had been thrown together because there had been no other option.

We continued to correspond. He continued to call, sporadically. School just was not what I wanted. I was lost in my life, had no sense of purpose, and couldn't focus on my studies. I was waiting for a reason to *be*. The more I heard from Eric, the more I heard about Billy, the more I thought my destiny was to be with them. After all, I loved children and hoped one day to have six of my own. While living at home and recovering from anorexia, I taught preschool and studied child development at George Mason University. Certainly I could help Eric with Billy. I was confident that I could take care of Billy and be the mother he needed but never had the chance to have. I never thought that he just might not want me.

Eric invited me to fly to Germany for spring break. Even though I was not fond of flying, I didn't give it a second thought. I immediately began to plan my trip. I researched cheap airfares and increased my baby-sitting so that I could earn enough money to buy my ticket. I took the steps needed to obtain a passport. I had never been out of the United States, in fact the farthest west I had been was Minnesota. Under normal circumstances, flying across the ocean would have scared me, but since that Christmas day in 1985, nothing seemed to scare me anymore.

Eric and I wrote frequent letters back and forth between that Christmas and spring break of 1985. His communications made it obvious to me that he was having a rough time taking care of Billy, working, and keeping things together. My sister, Patti, was the president of the Delta Delta Delta sorority at Virginia Tech. She and my brother, Phil, a Sigma Chi, encouraged me to get involved socially at Tech. They meant well. I just could not get myself motivated to be a college student.

Eric's letters became more intense, and I became more uncomfortable with my life as a college student. Eric told me in his letters that Billy needed a mother. Although I had never shared my desire to have six children with anyone, I began baby-sitting at the age of ten. I was always "so" responsible. I had taught preschool and took college-level child development courses. In my mind, I was ready to be a mother. I wasn't a good student anymore, surely, I could be a good mother. Billy needed one.

Eric asked me to marry him in a hand-written letter, using a kid-like type of code. He wrote the message in numbers and assigned a letter to each number. It was simple, it was sweet, and I was hooked. Without hesitating. I said yes and began to pack my clothes and mail my things to Germany. I withdrew from Virginia Tech, and in my mind, began to plan my new role as military wife and mother. I did all of these things without thinking and without telling anyone . . . except Eric.

Knowing him like I do now, I am shocked that he actually showed up at the Frankfurt airport to pick me up. We had only been together four days. He had been forced to be a dad, and I was lost in a life of uncertainty and self-doubt. He needed a mom for Billy. I needed a reason for being. We were a match made of nothing more than sheer desperation. Desperate matches do not have a future. Desperate matches lead to turmoil and broken hearts. I put all of my hope on Eric's representations to me that he loved me and that we, together, would build a family. As an enlisted member of the Air Force, he would never make a lot of money, but money had never mattered to me. I knew we would not have much, but I never expected to end up living on welfare, either.

The military housing complex where Eric lived was nestled in the quaint German town of Nieder Roden. The scenery could have been the set for *The Sound of Music*. It was charming and pretty. Eric's apartment was on the thirteenth floor, and the view from the apartment was lovely. The German countryside was lush and green.

It was a time of concern for U.S. citizens staying in Germany. Tensions between the United States and Libya were high. Car bombs had exploded in parking garages used by American military families. Military dependents were warned to "try to not look" too American. Normally, the circumstances would have made me feel unsafe and uneasy, but, while I was there, in a completely foreign country, with no means of independent support, I felt OK. I suppose because I felt instantly needed.

Upon my arrival, I immediately became the mother to an obviously troubled three-year-old little boy. The day after I got to Germany, Eric headed off to work at 5:30 A.M., leaving Billy and me to fend for ourselves. The apartment building was adjacent to a small community center, which eventually became my refuge and my place to escape from the troubles that went on in the thirteenth-floor apartment. I soon found young, military mothers to be my friends. I also met a wonderful, middle-aged couple, Martha and Mac, who became my surrogate parents while I was in Germany. They had known Kelly, they knew Eric, and they knew Billy. Martha and Mac became my best resources and my best allies.

I learned about Eric and Kelly's volatile history while I spent time with Martha and Mac. They loved Billy, and hoped that I could step in and become a mother to him. Billy's mother made no effort to contact him in Germany, and the childcare center on the base had difficulty dealing with Billy's resultant bad behavior. Eric had been late or had sometimes even missed work because of Billy's troubles. I quickly learned that I was supposed to be the answer. I was supposed to be Billy's saving grace.

Billy's sleep schedule was erratic and upside down. He would stay awake until all hours of the night and didn't nap regularly, and as a result, he was often irritable and unkind to other children. He had a hard time playing with other children and was aggressive and always wanted things for himself. He became easily frustrated when disciplined. But, Billy was just a little boy. He was lonely, angry, and obviously missing his mother.

Eric's mother, Carol, called me frequently and expressed her relief that I was there with Billy. She knew firsthand about Eric's irresponsibility, Kelly's lack of interest in Billy, and Billy's obvious emotional problems. Carol relied on my being there to take care of Billy. If I was taking care of Billy, then, she didn't have to take over the responsibility.

I worked daily with Billy, trying to give him structure, stability, friends, appropriate social activities, a little bit of preschool education, and unconditional love. He was so needy. He had been born to a mother who was still a child and a father who behaved like one. On Easter Sunday, 1986, I called my parents in Virginia and told them I wouldn't be returning home at the end of spring break. Looking back, I believe my mom knew then that I wouldn't return to Virginia Tech. My dad, however, was another story. Just as I had when I left college because of anorexia, I was disappointing him again by refusing to return to Virginia. He threatened to fly to Germany and drag me home. He even threatened to call the military and have Eric's first sergeant force me to leave. In the end, he did none of those things. I was, after all, almost twenty-two years old. No one could force me to do anything I didn't want to do. I gave up an entirely paid-for college education and all the security of the family that had raised me . . . all for a tragic, blondehaired little boy and his errant, childlike father.

After two months, word got to Eric's commander that I was living in the military housing. Although I did not know it at the time, Eric was ordered to either marry me, or send me home. Of course, Eric never told me about his commander's ultimatum, Martha told me after the wedding, during a shower she and some other friends had for me. I quickly assimilated into the life of military spouse. I cared for Billy, took care of the apartment, made the meals, did the laundry, taught aerobics and started a preschool program at the community center, and thought that, although Eric came home every night and fell asleep on the couch, I had a true purpose. I was comfortable, and I was needed.

In early July 1986, I discovered I was pregnant. I was scared, but, again, it was OK. Eric and I decided to tell Billy together. One late summer evening, after we cooked out on the grill and played basketball with some friends, we sat in the living room and told Billy that he would soon be having a brother or sister. It was at that moment that my hope of having found my purpose in life was shattered. Billy shouted that he didn't want a brother or a sister, and he screamed that if we brought a baby home, he would throw "it" off the balcony. We were thirteen stories up. I never expected his reaction, and I was frightened by it. That unexpected reaction turned out to be just the beginning of years of emotional turmoil and unrest.

Billy's reaction to my pregnancy quickly got out of control. He started to hit me in the stomach, and one early morning as I slept on the couch, I was awakened from a deep sleep to find Billy standing over me with a pair of scissors in his hands. He had cut up his bed. He painted the bathroom red in the middle of the night, using fingerpaints that were kept on top of the refrigerator. He was cruel to our cat and abusive to other kids. Although it was his son who was out of control, Eric ignored the problems. He was never awake when he was home, and he refused to discuss what was going on. I consulted with the base psychologist, who concluded that he was not equipped with the professional expertise to help Billy with the deeply embedded emotional pain he was expressing.

Billy took out his pain on me, and I didn't know how to handle it. I was too afraid to sleep and became exhausted. Every day was a battle with a very angry child. Nothing seemed to help Billy—no words of reassurance or promises that a brother or a sister would be a good thing. Billy's rage increased, and I miscarried my first child in late August 1986.

Things with Billy continued to deteriorate. Eric's income was not sufficient to meet our expenses, so I got a part-time job at the base hotel. Billy went back to the base child care center while I worked. After a few weeks, I discovered I was pregnant again. My morning sickness became a problem, and I had to quit my job at the hotel. Eric was informed by the child care center that Billy was not welcome there because of his bad behavior. One evening, when Eric was in Belgium on a temporary assignment, I went to see a movie at the community center with my friend Lynette. She and I hired a teenage baby-sitter to watch Billy and Lynette's daughter, Nicole. As Lynette and I walked across the cement courtyard, between the community center and the apartment building, we looked up, to our horror, and saw Billy hanging out of his window, thirteen stories up. I raced toward the building, ran up the stairs, ran into the apartment, grabbed Billy from the window sill, and gave him a spanking I will never forget. He had removed a dresser drawer and made makeshift stairs up to the window sill. Billy had almost fallen out of that window. Enough was enough. I called Eric in a panic and explained what happened. As usual, he was not worried. As usual, he was not there and had no appreciation for the seriousness of what could have happened that night. Our family was about to fall apart, so I did the only thing I could. I called my parents and asked for permission to come home. They agreed, so I took Billy with me, left Eric in Germany, and went state-side so I could get professional help for Billy and proper medical care for the baby I was carrying.

I took Billy to the psychiatrist who had treated me for anorexia. At the time, he was considered to be the best, and I wanted the best for Billy. We had a long road ahead of us. Dr. McMurrer, the psychiatrist, diagnosed Billy with hyperactivity and attention deficit disorder. He prescribed medication, and Billy began to improve. His sleep schedule and his behavior improved, and things overall were getting better.

I got a job at a local bank, and my mom watched Billy while I worked. Eric stayed in Germany. We kept the news about the new baby from Billy until the psychiatrist determined that the time was right to tell him. Emotionally, it was difficult for me to be away from Eric. But, as a practical matter, it was easier to take care of Billy and work and do what was needed to save our family without Eric with us. Billy's psychiatric treatment uncovered the possibility that he had been subjected to physical and emotional abuse. Dr. McMurrer saw us once a week and recommended that Eric get out of the service so that Billy could remain state-side and continue to get the psychiatric care he needed. We did.

Eric was granted a hardship discharge in the spring of 1987. He packed up our things in Germany, including our two cats and their four kittens, and we found a tiny townhouse in Virginia. I continued to work at the bank, and Billy continued in counseling. Eric found a job with a local grocery chain, and I thought we were at last on our way to some sense of normalcy. I was wrong. When baby Phillip arrived, Billy's reaction was worse than I ever imagined. He cut up his quilt with a knife within twenty-four hours of my bringing Phillip home from the hospital. Billy's behavior terrified me. My baby was brand new, and Billy wanted to hurt him. When Billy articulated his desire to do so, I called the psychiatrist in a panic. He saw us right away and advised me that Billy should stay with someone else while he had time to adjust to having to share me with a new baby brother. That night, I had a panic attack in the bathroom. I was so scared. I thought I was having a heart attack. No one wanted to take Billy. I tracked down Kelly, and she told me that she was afraid of Billy and that she just could not take care of him. Neither set of grandparents wanted to take him, not even for a few weeks while we all adjusted to the new situation. We ended up in court, where the court services officer informed us all that if someone did not take Billy, he would have to go into foster care. Finally, Eric's parents agreed to take Billy. We were all ordered to have evaluations and to engage in counseling. I did my part, but my in-laws refused to follow through with counseling. Instead, they hired an attorney, had both Kelly and Eric sign away their parental rights, and, angrily, kept Billy with them . . . permanently.

Four

Deadbeat Dads and Alienating Moms

At the heart of America's welfare problem are parents, rather persons, who have produced children but cannot, or will not, see beyond their own individual wants and desires. These people allow their children to go without food, shelter, clothing, medical care, and other necessities without wondering how, or who, will care for their kids. Welfare is not about adults who are too lazy to work. Welfare is about adults who walk away from their children.

A federal campaign to reduce the rate of teenage pregnancy in the United States, includes the use of a billboard that depicts an adorable, blue-eyed, caucasian baby looking cute and loveable. At the top of the billboard is printed the caption, "A baby costs $785 a month. How much is your allowance?" Clearly, the intent of the billboard message is to discourage teenagers from having babies.

However, the $785 a month figure suggested by the billboard represents approximately 685 percent of the amount the government pays in welfare assistance for one child! When my family received "welfare," the monthly check for five children was approximately $573. According to the government estimate captioned on the billboard, $3,925 is the monthly cost of five children. The government's welfare payment was $3,352 short.

Welfare is not a windfall. The amount provided by government public assistance checks falls far below the amount necessary to take care of a child. Welfare is neither intended, nor sufficient, to cover the basic needs of a family. It is never enough money to cover food, shelter, clothing, medicine, baby formula, and the requirements of daily living. The widely held public perception that welfare provides a "free" and "easy" ride for adults in the system is plainly, and clearly, wrong.

Pursuant to the requirements of federal and state law's, general "welfare" payments are available to custodial parents of children who are not being supported by an absent parent, a parent who does not live in the family household. Public assistance is not for parents who live together in a family unit. Public assistance money is not "free" money.

Contrary to what is commonly believed, a complete government accounting is kept of any and all money's paid to a family through welfare programs. The sum total of this money is called a "debt to state." It is not free money. The "debt to state" is expected, and in theory sought, to be paid back to the government by the absent parent.

As determined by Title IV-D of the Social Security Act of the United States Code, child support enforcement agencies are charged with the task of collecting and recouping welfare money. Sadly, the government's collection rate for the recoupment of public assistance funds is limited to approximately 13 percent. Overall, child support collection rates across the country range from 23 percent to 37 percent. Too many children in the United States today go without their child support. Too many parents in the United States today ignore their obligations to pay child support and leave their children in a circumstance of financial neglect.

For many children, Father's Day is a painful reminder of a gaping void. According to assorted studies and surveys, approximately one-third of the children in the United States today are living in homes without dads. Evidence of this statistic is too often provided by the fifteen-year-old car jacker living angrily on inner city streets, or, by the soft-spoken nine-year-old girl who refuses to smile because her dad left her when she was five years old. The images are poignant, and all too familiar.

How did this trend of absent fathers become so prevalent? There are probably many reasons, however, one of the most blatant—and most forgotten—is the United States Supreme Court case of *Planned Parenthood of Central Missouri v. Danforth*. In *Dan-*

forth, the Court held that a Missouri statute, which required the consent of a married father when his spouse sought an abortion of their unborn child, was unconstitutional. In one stroke of the pen, the Court determined that fathers, in the United States, are irrelevant.

If the highest court in the land holds that a father has no legal right to veto his wife's abortion of their unborn child, how can all of the lower courts require those same fathers to pay child support? Even more disturbing would be the flip side of the *Danforth* decision. Could it logically lead to a father's legal argument that his wife should have an abortion because he does not desire to have the child? The implications of the *Danforth* decision could be far-reaching and scary. But more importantly, what impact has this 1976 decision had on the state of fatherhood in the United States today?

Of course, fathers are not irrelevant. Most states carry statutes that read, "a child is entitled to the benefit and support of both parents." Unfortunately, in today's society, the value of fatherhood and the traditional "two-parent" family has been minimized, even trivialized. In our country today, there exists a cultural climate of disintegrating families and rising rates of divorce. As a society, we need a new sense of commitment. We need a renewed passion for the benefits and stability of family life. These are qualities that cannot be legislated . . . qualities that no law, no rule, no ordinance, no statute can provide. These qualities must come from the hearts of parents and must focus on the well-being and the best interests of our children.

Of those parents who desert their children and families, leaving those children and families to turn to welfare to meet their basic needs, approximately 85 percent are never held accountable. Which means that only 15 percent of those parents ever pay child support. Noncustodial, or absent, parents offer numerous and varied excuses as to why they cannot pay their child support. Neither do these parents typically offer solutions for meeting their children's needs.

"You can't get blood from a turnip," is a statement that has become a motto of parents who purposefully avoid their child support obligations. Common excuses for failure to pay support include unemployment, underemployment, the need to pay for new family and/or children, disagreement about how the mother of the

child(ren) should spend the money, not having the visitation schedule desired, not having enough money for him or herself, and simply not wanting to give any money to the "other parent," even if that money is intended to support a child. It is disgraceful that adults in a country as affluent and educated as ours would try to rationalize their willful failure to financially care for their children as a justifiable withholding of money from the adult who represents a relationship gone bad.

Just as there are "deadbeat dads" who refuse to support their kids, there are also alienating moms who often contribute to the toxic circumstances that lead to a parent's failure to pay child support. It is easy for a deserted parent to express anger and frustration in front of the kids toward the parent that walked away. I know, because I have done it myself, on many occasions.

It is tough to remain cheerful and positive about a man who walked out and left you and your children to survive on food stamps. It is difficult to be both mom and dad for any child, and the difficulty often leads to resentment, disgust, and a desire for the other parent to disappear from the lives of the children. Instead of seeking counseling and appropriate methods of dealing with this type of anger and resentment, some abandoned parents engage themselves, and their children, in a systematic attempt to alienate that other parent from his or her children.

There is a syndrome called "parental alienation," which can cause severe psychological damage to the children involved and can result in irreparable harm to the relationships between those children and their absent parents. Some deserted, custodial parents carry enormous hurt and pain after being left alone to care for and raise a child or children. In my work as a family law attorney, I have encountered this syndrome on numerous occasions. Sometimes the alienation is subtle; sometimes it teeters on the brink of being criminal.

To gain leverage in a custody suit, it is not uncommon for one parent to report the other parent to social services, accusing them of neglect or abuse. The most devastating of such allegations are those involving sexual abuse. Sadly, unwarranted claims of neglect and abuse are frequently found in the court files of ugly, heated

custody battles. One parent accuses the other of abuse, hoping to keep that other parent away, from the children.

I have encountered parents who have fabricated allegations against each other and I have discovered evidence that some parents coach their children into believing untrue things about the other parent. I have been approached with scenarios concerning abuse and neglect that can't be substantiated. It is a horrible violation of the legal process when such things occur. It is a more horrible violation of the children involved and generally throws them into lives of turmoil, uncertainty, and a seemingly never-ending tornado of court hearings and legal proceedings. No children should be subject to such destructive circumstances because of their parents' efforts to obliterate each other. Thankfully, many judges will not tolerate cases that turn down the twisted path of parental alienation. Judges have and will continue to remove children from both parents in cases where the battle between the adults becomes more important than the best interests of the children.

The problem of "deadbeat dads" will never be resolved. The Personal Responsibility and Work Opportunity Act requires that a remedy calling for revocation of driver's, professional, occupational, and recreational licenses be established and authorized by states for use in the courts. Also, some states choose to impose jail terms for noncustodial parents who refuse to pay child support. And, any parent who fails to obey a court order to pay support could be jailed for contempt of court. However, an incarcerated parent is not a working parent. Therefore, while the parent is incarcerated, his or her debt continues to rise and the child or children continue to go without needed support. Although some jurisdictions allow nonpaying parents to participate in work-release programs, where they are allowed to leave lockup during the day for work, most do not, because such release programs are expensive to operate and oversee.

There is no easy answer, and there are no creative solutions. Sadly, legislation cannot change the hearts of parents who freely abandon their children and leave them without the financial support they require. No politician can make this problem go away. The best we can do, as a society, is loudly, persistently, aggressively, and incessantly refuse to tolerate people who walk out on their kids.

We cannot passively accept such behavior. We cannot allow such behavior to be the subject of "cute" situation comedies or trendy movies. We cannot turn our heads the other way when people of power abandon their families. As a culture, as a unified nation, we must speak up and put a stop to parental desertion. It hurts our children, our most vulnerable. It hurts our government by putting an enormous drain on resources and by creating unnecessary bureaucracies. And, it hurts our economy, by requiring the use of taxpayer funds to meet the needs of children who should be provided for by their parents.

Five

He Has a Right to Privacy

Two weeks before the night Eric left for good, on May 16, 1990, he and I attended a wedding together. Things had been difficult, but it had been almost five months since he had last left and returned home. He had taken a flight to St. Louis intending to never return, but after deplaning in a city totally unknown to him, he got scared and flew back. I was almost five months pregnant with baby number four. Then one night, after pretending to go to work at his part-time delivery job, Eric grabbed his prepacked suitcase and ran out the door. I followed him screaming and grabbing on the hood of the car—our only car.

Two years earlier, when I was eight months pregnant with April, my first daughter and second child, Eric spent six weeks in Dominion Psychiatric Hospital for depression and a seizure disorder. His team of doctors and social workers met with me and strongly suggested that I move on. They implied that my children and I would be better off without him in our lives and that, unless he accepted responsibility for his depression, took his medicine, and followed through with counseling, he would never be a responsible husband and father. Although I was certain I could "save him," I made the decision to complete my undergraduate degree, just in case I had to support my family on my own.

While at the psychiatric hospital, I met Karen, the first of a series of girlfriends Eric would have during the course of our marriage. Although their relationship was not physical, it might as well have been. Eric had a habit of connecting to unsuspecting women. He would share with them a tale of woe, never tell them about our young children, and always portray me as a selfish, nagging, horrible, money-hungry wife. With his large, brown eyes and sad story, Eric had a pathetic charm about him that attracted all types of women. Young, middle-aged, almost fifty. It didn't seem to matter. Eric was like a magnet for codependent women. I was, and probably still am, the worst offender of them all.

Our marriage survived that hospitalization. Eric returned home. He took his medication and went to counseling. As long as he was taking his medication for depression, things went well for us. Our two young children were progressing well, and I completed my undergraduate degree. I worked part time as a bank teller. We were not rich, but, I thought we were happy. At least I was.

During the fall of 1988, I returned to teaching preschool. My mom watched the babies while I taught class every morning. I loved working with children. My heart still ached when I thought about Billy, but I tried to channel that pain into helping other children. In April 1989, it became apparent that Eric had stopped taking his medication. He began to have angry outbursts and started going in late for work. I caught him drinking beer early in the morning hours after finishing a night shift. Eric yelled at me whenever I tried to talk to him about his medication. One morning, when I was pregnant with our second daughter, Tricia, I counted his pills and discovered that he was days behind, and I confronted him about it. He punched me in the eye. Not directly, but it was close enough. I went to the local magistrate and filed a warrant for spousal abuse. Eric was arrested and released on his own recognizance. We went to family court; it was my first court experience.

We worked with a court mediator named Jerry Rich in Fairfax County's Juvenile and Domestic Relations Court. Eric pled guilty to misdemeanor assault and was ordered to complete a program of probation for one year. The probation included regular monitoring of his medication and frequent meetings with his probation officer. This supervision worked well for a short period of time. But, when the probation officer stopped calling, Eric stopped following the court's order. Again, things got worse.

The roof of the townhouse we rented began to leak severely. Although Eric was working regularly, and we had small, but steady income, the problems related to the house became more than I could manage. Eric worked night shifts as a stock clerk for Shopper's Food Warehouse. He never did well on an overnight work schedule. He generally arrived home several hours after his shift ended, after drinking beer with his fellow workers out in the store parking lot. He never went out, at least not that I knew of, so I thought I should let him do something with his friends. Besides, with two infants and a baby on the way, I was too tired to fight.

That late spring and early summer were wet and humid. The twenty-year-old townhouse we rented was in desperate need of roof repairs. Water gathered on the flat rooftop and slowly oozed down the drywall into the inner structure of the house. New, large watermarks appeared every day. When the dryer ran, the house filled with dust, and the smoke alarm went off. One particular evening, while I was fixing supper in the kitchen, I looked up and noticed that the commode from the upstairs bathroom was about to fall through the floor directly onto my kitchen cabinets and counters.

In a panic, I called my landlord, Mr. Marshall. He and his wife were retirees, living in Punta Gorda, Florida. Of course there was not a whole lot they could do from Florida about the crisis that was about to occur in my kitchen, but I called and informed them nonetheless. Mr. Marshall assured me that he would call a plumber to come out to the house and take a look at the problem. Several weeks passed without any sign of a plumber. Day by day, the water stain that formed the outline of the commode increased in size and darkness. It was just a matter of time before that toilet would end up on my kitchen counter. Water stains became increasingly visible all around the house. Stains ran from the ceilings down to the floors. The carpets near the doors and windows were soaked, causing the house to smell of mold and of dog urine from previous tenants. It was the final straw for me, when swarms of termites began to appear under the living room and kitchen lights every evening after dark.

I contacted the Fairfax County Tenant-Landlord Commission for help. The office sent me a booklet about tenant/landlord rights and responsibilities. I read through the book and discovered that the water and insect problems were serious enough to warrant the termination of my lease if Mr. Marshall didn't repair the leaks within thirty days. Although I was not a lawyer, I wrote a brief letter informing Mr. Marshall about the leak and the bugs, demanding that repairs be made within thirty days, and further, letting him know that if all repairs were not made in a timely manner as required by the law, our lease would be terminated. I sent the letter via certified mail and began my quest for an alternate place to live.

The summer of 1989 was a slow summer for the rental market in Fairfax County. New apartment buildings were opening all over the county, so competition for new tenants was keen. Every complex offered some type of incentive to entice new applicants. I found a lovely, new, two-level, three-bedroom apartment in Centreville, Virginia. The unit overlooked the swimming pool and had a porch-like room that had floor to ceiling windows. When I saw that room, I knew it would be ideal as a children's playroom. In addition, the complex offered a full month of free rent. A month of free rent was like an answer to my prayers. I immediately applied, the application was accepted, and I began to make plans to move.

Mr. Marshall did nothing to fix the house. On the advice of the Tenant-Landlord Commission, I called the county health department. A health inspector came out to the property and immediately condemned it. The department contacted Mr. Marshall and informed him that he had seven days to comply with their code requirements regarding water leaks and sagging structure, but he failed to comply. We moved out June 30, 1989. Eric was not much help moving into the new apartment. His sleep schedule was so out of whack that most of the time he was not coherent enough to do much, so my mom and I moved most of our things. Unfortunately, our two-story unit was not ready on the move-in date, so we were put in an adjacent unit until ours was ready. This, of course, meant two moves. But, at least we were out of the house that had become become a horrible health hazard. Our daughter Tricia was born six days later.

In July of 1989, several weeks after Tricia was born, Eric moved out and lived in the local city of Manassas Park with a seventy-some-year-old woman. His stay there lasted approximately six weeks, and I didn't hear from him for two weeks after he left. In a panic, and without money or any means of support, I made my first contact with the Fairfax County Department of Social Services. I received a thick packet of information in the mail, filled out every piece of paperwork included, and immediately returned the package, hoping for a quick response. No response was forthcoming.

One day, during a busy morning of the housecleaning, the kids and I decided to take a break and go outside for a walk. We went upstairs to get light jackets for everyone, and the four of us, April, Phillip, Tricia, and I, walked down the stairs together. April first. Followed by Phillip. Me last, carrying Tricia. Somehow, April fell down the last couple of steps. She was carrying her blanket, and it seemed to have gotten caught under her feet, causing her to trip. I could tell by the way she was crying that something pretty serious had occurred. The way she held her arm, I figured that she had likely broken it. I called Eric at the number I had for him, but, he didn't answer, so I put the kids in the car and drove to the emergency room. Thankfully, we had good health insurance through the Local Union 400—we had always had good health insurance after leaving the military.

When we arrived at the hospital parking lot, I put Tricia and Phillip in the stroller and tried to carry April, as I pushed the stroller toward the emergency room door. April's crying had subsided substantially, but her arm didn't look right. We signed in with the triage nurse and sat down to wait to check in at the admissions desk. We waited about an hour before we were called. Phillip and Tricia stayed in the stroller, while I held April on my lap. The admissions clerk was kind while asking general questions about our address, insurance, April's age, health history, and so on. Everything seemed to be going OK, until the clerk called the insurance company to verify coverage for an emergency room visit. After the clerk placed the call I watched as her face changed from a pleasant to a puzzled expression. I knew that something was wrong.

After hanging up, the clerk gently informed me that we had no insurance. Eric, the insured, my husband, the kids' father, had been terminated more than a month earlier. The insurance had expired. We were not covered, and I panicked. April probably had a broken arm, and I had no money or insurance. But, she needed care. Overcome with emotion, I spilled my entire story to the clerk, who must have taken pity on us. She agreed to bill me later and advised me to apply for Medicaid for the kids as soon as possible. Medicaid, she explained, was the state's medical assistance program. Hopefully, we would qualify, and the bill would be covered retroactively. Hopefully. Hopefully.

April had a broken arm. She seemed so little to have a cast, but being little, her bones were soft, and the doctor assured me that she would heal quickly. After this incident, after discovering that Eric had no job, no insurance, and who knew what else was going on with him, I sank into a deep despair. I turned to my wonderful friend Ruby for help and encouragement. Ruby was a member of an aerobics class I taught at the Prison Fellowship Ministry in Reston, Virginia. I had become an aerobics instructor for Body and Soul, Inc., in 1984, as a sort of spiritual, emotional, and physical therapy for myself, while I was recovering from anorexia. I taught part time at different churches and other locations in Northern Virginia. Ruby was a faithful member of my Reston class. I never knew quite why, but Ruby made a real effort to befriend me. I guess she noticed my stress, or had some special sense about what was going on with me. She was a wonderful support—she helped me with laundry, with the kids, and just spent time talking with me, encouraging me to have faith, pray a lot, and stay the course with regard to Eric and our marriage.

Ruby and her husband, Tim, came over to the apartment and set me up with their church for help with our immediate needs. The wonderful youth group at the church came over to our home and played with the children, helped me clean, and brought us cloth diapers plus a month's supply of diaper detergent, rubber pants, and a new diaper pail. I was very humbled by the help we received. My sister was a summer associate at a large law firm, and she generously paid the rent for me for the month after Eric left. With her payment of the rent and the help from the church, we were OK . . . for a while.

I received a notice from the county that I had been approved for a general relief check . . . a one-time cash payment to provide some assistance to us following Eric's desertion. Along with the approval notice, I got a letter informing me that we would not be considered for any additional assistance until I supplied them with birth certificates and social security cards for me and each of the children. Getting ahold of all of those documents would be a task in itself.

I continued to try to contact Eric. I regularly spoke with the woman he lived with, who was elderly, soft-spoken, and over the telephone, seemed to be a caring person. It was obvious that Eric had not been forthcoming with her about our family circumstances. After we spoke several times, she began to call me to let me know what Eric was up to. One morning, she called in a panic, saying that Eric had left her home in the middle of the night. Hearing a loud noise around four in the morning, she woke up and was startled to see Eric taking his suitcases and other items out the front door. When she asked him what he was doing, he told her that he had a flight to catch and was going to St. Louis for a job interview.

Later that day, I discovered what had happened and who had made it possible. Eric's brother Derrick, my sister Patti's former, longtime boyfriend, was convinced that their break-up had been my fault and seemed determined to make my life miserable. At four o'-clock that afternoon, Derrick dropped Eric off on our doorstep and told him to get his act together, because he was finished trying to help him. When I saw Eric at the door, I was completely confused. Between the call from Eric's landlord and his appearance at the door later that same day, I felt as if I were stuck in some strange time warp. I would not let Eric into the apartment until he explained what was going on. I knew it was unlikely that I would get the truth, but I had to ask.

The alleged story was that Eric had had a job interview in St. Louis, for which Derrick had purchased the airplane ticket for Eric to travel. Although Eric could not, or would not, tell me what type of job interview it was, he said that he got there, got scared, hopped back on the next available plane, and returned to Virginia. Derrick picked him up at the airport and took him back to the woman's home in Manassas, but she wouldn't allow him back in her home. She was certain that he was trying to skip out on her. She would not let it happen again. Eric left her with a $350 telephone bill. He moved home with us, and I paid the bill.

Eric filed and qualified for unemployment compensation. It was not much money, but the approximately $198 per week was more than we'd had when Eric was in the Air Force. Although I was angry with him for making more messes that I had to clean up, I was relieved that he was home although I'm not sure why I was relieved. Eric had to get a job. The holidays were approaching, and United Parcel Service was hiring seasonal truck drivers. The pay was a minimum of $440 per week, plus lots of opportunities for overtime.

Eric was hired immediately and he brought home more than $500 a week. We had a wonderful Christmas. He worked from eight in the morning through six or seven each evening. The kids and I drove him to the UPS depot in the morning and picked him up in the evening. We ate dinner as a family, and for the first time, ever, we had enough money to pay our bills. Things were going well, and then, Eric was laid off.

UPS laid off all seasonal workers. Although Eric had received excellent performance reports, he was laid off near the middle of January, when the parcel delivery business began to slow down after the holidays. Eric was promised a permanent driver position with the company, however, due to the company's policy regarding seniority, and, because of Eric's recent date of hire, others would be offered permanent status first. We waited a week, then two, then four, then six. Finally, we could wait no longer. We had no money coming in. The rent was due. Unemployment ran out. Our brief period of family harmony had come to an end.

Six

Have You Tried Social Services?

It was painfully obvious. We were alone with no car, no money, no milk, no hope that he would return. In a panic, I opened the Yellow Pages and dialed every attorney who advertised a "free initial consultation." Of course, "free" doesn't always mean free. I talked to twenty attorneys and got twenty demands for three thousand dollars, or more, to serve as an initial retainer fee for my "kind of case." I had no money and an eviction notice from my apartment manager. I needed a lawyer, but, at that point, I couldn't even afford a "free" consultation.

I had a five-day "pay or quit" notice from the management of my apartment complex. We had gotten this type of notice before. We usually paid our rent after the fifth of each month, because our finances were so tight. But, we had always managed to gather the money and have the rent paid before the tenth of each month. Things had been tight, but after living with enlisted military pay, we had learned how to manage. Now, though, with three babies and one on the way, no job, no money, and no car, I was at a loss.

I couldn't tell my family. When I made the choice to stay in Germany and left my parents and my family in despair about my decision, I gave up my right to ask them for help. I had to find Eric. After the UPS, and six weeks of unemployment, Eric took a job as a plumber's apprentice in Washington, D.C. I called the plumbing shop. I tried to appeal to the office manager's sense of compassion when I asked her for Eric's new address. Being a woman, I hoped that she would help me out, but no such help was forthcoming. I called the take-out service where Eric worked part time, and pleaded with Eric's supervisor to help me find him. But he wouldn't give me any information, either. Nothing at all.

When he left, Eric took a suitcase, a small bag, and, oddly, our cable television converter box. The next morning, I fed the kids, put on videotapes for Phillip and April, put Tricia in her swing, and began to develop a plan. I had to find Eric, but I couldn't call his family. After Eric's parents took legal custody of Billy and refused to help us follow through with counseling, our communication had stopped.

I walked around the apartment and looked in the closets and all the places where Eric kept his things. Everything, except a few items of clothing, was still in its place. But, he had taken the cable box. I realized that box was the key to locating Eric. If he had taken the box, he must be using the service, too. I called Media General Cable and asked the customer service person to tell me the address where Eric had transferred our service. To my surprise and increased frustration, the customer service representative refused to give me any information about the service transfer. She told me that the information was confidential. Even though I was on the account, had paid the bills, and gave her all of my personal information, she would not help me. Eric had a right to privacy. I wasn't going to get any help from Media General Cable.

Just about exasperated, with five dollars in my purse and no idea what to do next, I sat down on the family room floor and fell apart. Thankfully, Phillip and April played quietly. They didn't notice what I was doing. Fortunately, they were too young to understand that their daddy had abandoned them. Fortunately, they were too young to understand that my life was in turmoil even though their needs continued uninterrupted. My children were my saving grace. They were then, and they continue to be now. When I was ready to give up in despair, someone needed a diaper change, or a new bottle of juice, or a cracker, or something—some need sufficient to draw me out of my haze of worry.

It came to me while I sat there on the cream-colored carpet. The cable company was my only avenue to finding Eric. If I couldn't get the information directly, surely there had to be another way. And, there was. I called Media General a second time, hoping I wouldn't get the same customer service representative on the line. Thankfully, this time, it was a different person. After he asked how he could be of help and verified my account number, I explained that we were moving and that I wanted to be sure that the cable company had my new address and telephone number in their system. Without any further inquiry, the gentleman read off a Centreville, Virginia, street address and telephone number. I quickly thanked him for his help and hung up the phone.

I stared at the address I had written down. Not overly familiar with Centreville, I had no idea where this "Summer Pond Drive" was. Knowing that the police nonemergency line could help me locate the address, I called to get directions. That call was uneventful, and I was able to get door to door instructions. Then, I went back to the Yellow Pages and found the number of the closest taxicab company. I called the company and asked what the fare would be from my apartment to the Centreville address. I dressed the kids, put a diaper bag together, called a cab, checked to be certain that my $5 was still in my purse, got everyone together, and took everyone outside to wait.

It was about forty-five minutes before the cab arrived, and the kids got a bit fussy waiting outside on the steps in front of the apartment. When the cab got there, car seats and all, we climbed into the cab. The driver knew exactly how to find the address, and he quoted the fare at approximately $4.75. I had just enough money for a 25-cent tip and no return trip, but enough to get there.

We pulled up to a prefab-type apartment complex. The kind that looks as if it were pieced together like a three-dimensional jigsaw puzzle. The apartment units surrounded a lake. It was a nice place. My heart started to pound in my chest as the cab pulled up in front of the address I had scratched on the envelope of an overdue electric bill. The driver opened the doors for me and the kids, removed the three car seats from the cab, and carefully lined them up on the sidewalk, one after the other. I gave him my last five dollars. He asked me if he should wait for us, and I explained that I had no more money, thanked him for his kindness, and apologized for the tiny tip. He wished us luck and left.

I carried Tricia and encouraged April and Phillip to walk up the two flights of steps to the apartment. My stomach felt sick. The kids were fussing. I was scared and angry and hurt. I had no idea who, or what, I would find on the other side of the apartment door. I knocked, and waited. To my surprise, Eric opened the door. When he saw us, he slammed the door shut. I knocked again, but there was no answer. I continued to knock, and Eric continued to refuse to answer. I started to cry and shouted for him to open the door, but still, he didn't answer.

After we had waited about half an hour, a delivery man appeared at the door with food for Eric and whoever else was inside the apartment with him. The delivery man knocked and shouted out who he was. The door opened. A woman stood in the doorway, paid the bill, took the food, and closed the door. The kids and I continued to wait, and I knocked every few minutes, to no avail. Finally, I pounded on the door, shouting for Eric to open it and talk to me. I asked where the car was. I asked for the keys and said I needed the car for the kids. He yelled back through the door to "go away" and threatened to call the police. By this time, I was sobbing uncontrollably. I had no way to get home and no money. The kids were crying. We were too far away from home to walk, and we had three car seats to carry.

I led the kids down the steps, and we sat on the sidewalk. I saw Eric and his woman friend watching us from the apartment balcony. By now, the kids were getting hungry, so I gave them some crackers and tried to get them to sit in their car seats on the sidewalk. I had no idea what to do. I desperately hoped that Eric would come down and help us but he didn't. I looked up through tears and saw a police car drive onto the street. The car stopped in front of the building. The officer looked at me and the kids and took the stairs up toward the apartment where Eric and the woman were. After a few minutes, the officer returned to his car, asked me who I was, and told me that Eric and the resident of the apartment wanted me to leave. I explained to the officer that Eric had deserted me and the kids, that we had no money, that he had our only automobile, and that we had no way to get home.

The officer's cruiser could not accommodate three car seats. I had no credit cards and not even enough change to make a telephone call. The officer informed me that although the kids and I were technically sitting on public sidewalks, we could, nonetheless, be asked to leave the premises. He said he would give us a ride home, but his car was too small. He asked if I had someone I could call. My parents didn't know about Eric's most recent, and most serious desertion. I just couldn't call them—at least not yet.

The officer climbed back behind the wheel of his car and drove off. After a few more minutes, the woman from upstairs came down. She introduced herself as Kelly and said she was separated from her husband and had a young daughter of her own. She had met Eric on the Metro Bus on the morning route into Washington, D.C. During our conversation, I found out that we had gone to Madison High School in Vienna, Virginia, together and that she did not know about all the kids and the baby on the way. Eric had portrayed me as a horrible nag of a wife who was always taking his money and demanding more. It was his normal course of behavior and typical description of me. Kelly was nice enough, and she drove me and the kids home. As I removed the last car seat from her car, I asked her to please make Eric move out of her apartment and come home. She closed the window and drove off.

Two days later, my parents and sister picked the children and me up to attend my sister's law school graduation ceremony at the University of Virginia. It was a very proud day for my folks. I was grateful to be offered a ride, because I still had no idea where the car was and couldn't bring myself to tell my parents that Eric had left, again. It was a good day. I didn't want to ruin it with another Eric-related drama. My sister became a lawyer that day, May 20, 1990, and my parents were very proud. The children were well-behaved. We stopped in Charlottesville and had something to eat before heading back to northern Virginia. It was a good day, but I still had to tell all three of them what happened.

After hearing my story, my dad offered to drive to Kelly's apartment complex so we could look for my car. My mom had an extra car key that I had made. If we found the car, I could use the extra key to take it. We pulled into the apartment complex and drove through the small parking lots adjacent to the building where Eric was staying. After only a few minutes, I spotted the car parked across the parking lot immediately in front of the building. We quickly put the car seats in the car, I thanked my parents, congratulated my sister, hopped in, and drove off. At least I had the car back. Keeping it would require some creativity, but I had a plan.

I pulled the car in front of our apartment. One by one, as I always did, I removed the kids from their car seats, and, individually, carried them upstairs. I could not carry all three children at once. I put Phillip and April in their cribs and set Tricia up in her swing. Then, I went back down to the car, drove it to the rear of the apartment complex, and parked it in a remote spot that could not be easily seen from the main street. I had to hide the car. I needed that car, and I couldn't let Eric take it away again.

I began to plan. I had to take care of the kids, and I had to go after Eric and force him to help us. I needed to find a new place to live, and I needed to buy food, pay bills, and seek prenatal care for the baby I was carrying. There was a lot to do. I needed to get family law advice, and I needed it fast and at no cost. The day my sister graduated from law school, the day I took the car back, was the day I realized that Eric was not going to help us. No amount of guilt was going to reach him. The kids and I were on our own.

Monday morning, at eight o'clock, I called the Fairfax County Juvenile and Domestic Relations Court intake office. It was the same office where I had filed a spousal abuse complaint the time Eric had given me a black eye before Tricia was born. The voice on the telephone was impatient and curt. I asked for an appointment, indicating I wanted to file petitions for child support, spousal support, and child custody, and I needed to do it immediately. The voice responded that the next available appointment was three weeks away. Frustrated, I asked if there was any way for me to be seen sooner. The receptionist told me that I could come in to the office and wait. If there happened to be a cancellation, I might be seen without an appointment. Desperate and determined, I packed up the kids, put everyone in the car, and headed off to the courthouse.

The kids and I went to the courthouse every day, for three days, before an intake officer could see us. Waiting in the office was hard on the kids. We waited for five or six hours each day. I packed juice and crackers and toys. Children are not meant to sit for long periods of time in waiting rooms, but, we had no choice. I finally filed my three petitions. Thankfully, I had Eric's address and social security number. Without those two pieces of information, I could not have filed anything.

The court clerk explained the process to me. Although the idea of going to court was scary, the idea of being evicted or going without food for the kids was unimaginable. I had no choice. I had to do whatever it took to get help. After the paperwork was neatly and completely filled out, the kids and I were directed back to the waiting room, a place that after three days, had become way too familiar, to wait to be assigned a court date.

A clerk brought me a tissue paper-like copy of the petitions, complete with a court date. When I read the date, my heart sank. August 23, 1990. August? It was May. What would we do for three months? In three months, we would be homeless. How would I buy food for the kids? How would I buy diapers and medicine? I couldn't ask my family for help. I had married Eric, I had made the choice, I had had the kids. I needed to figure it out. I started to cry as I gathered our things. My tears dripped on the bottles and the toys as I scooped them up from the floor and packed them back into the diaper bag. The clerk heard me sobbing and offered to help. She helped me put the kids in the stroller and asked if I had tried social services. I had never thought about it. I couldn't even imagine what a food stamp looked like. But, again, I had no choice.

Seven

Rush Is Wrong . . . Dr. Laura Is Right

In 1993, I attempted to start a support group for single parents at my Fairfax, Virginia, church. My church had been supportive and helpful to me and my children. But, churches can be tough places for single-parent families. Growing up, I had faithfully gone to church. I was raised as a Lutheran and found great comfort and stability in knowing and trusting in a power greater than myself, greater than any of us.

As a little girl, I dreamed about one day neatly filling a pew at church . . . my husband and me, bookends of sorts, with our neatly dressed and impeccably behaved children sitting quietly between us. My reality, which was the direct result of my choice to marry young, without really knowing the person I married, was that I went to church every Sunday, with all of the kids, but without my husband, and did my best to practice crowd and noise control within my own group of five kids. After a month or two of struggling to get through a service, it became apparent that the best way to keep the children going to church was for me to teach Sunday school and get as involved as I possibly could. That's what I did.

Organizing the support/study group for single parents was one of the things I attempted to do at church to bring people like me together. Being a single parent, especially a parent of small children, can be extremely lonely and isolating. Logic would fairly conclude that a single parent of multiple youngsters could never be lonely. However, having the sole responsibility to care and provide for another human being can be a most frightening and isolating experience. I looked for comrades in similar circumstances. Along the way, I met many.

One of the ladies in my first single-parent study group introduced me to the sense of companionship she felt listening to talk radio. During a break in our weekly study group meeting, she casually mentioned her addiction to talk radio, especially to those shows hosted by Rush Limbaugh and Dr. Laura Schlessinger. After several days of listening, I too became hooked. The radio became my sole source of adult companionship, and, for a while, my sole source of information, entertainment, and intellectual challenge.

Talk radio inspired the advocate in me. I often found myself talking back to the hosts of the shows, especially when they spoke of topics that were, painfully, a part of my daily life. Rush Limbaugh, a conservative talk show host, well-known and well-vilified, sparked my interest and my outrage when he frequently opened his show at twelve o'clock noon by welcoming all listeners, especially the "welfare recipients who were just getting out of bed." I was a welfare recipient when I first became a Rush regular.

Being a Rush regular involved listening to daily derogatory comments about the government's redistribution of wealth and incessant remarks about welfare recipients who attach themselves to the government's "nipple" and refuse to work for a living. I knew then and know now, that some people living "on the system" truly take improper advantage of every free resource they can find. Some lie to get food stamps and misrepresent their household composition to secure subsidized housing. But, "some" are not all. "Some" are not the majority.

Rush is wrong to overgeneralize the reality of public assistance in the United States today. Rush was wrong in 1995 and 1996, when, during the heat of the national welfare reform debate, he focused his discussions of welfare on people who just would not work and would not engage in taking care of themselves. In 1995 and 1996, the average family qualifying for and receiving a welfare check consisted of a married, white, twenty-six-year-old woman, with two young children. The average recipient was not a black, inner-city resident with twelve children and as many possible fathers. The average recipient was a mom like me, a married mom whose husband,

and the father of all of her children, chose to walk away and leave the government to take his place as provider.

As a lifelong conservative, I firmly believe that the government's role in the lives of its citizens should, and must, be limited. The beauty of American life is American freedom. This freedom allows us all to make choices . . . choices that might lead to circumstances that require government intervention. Holding parents accountable to provide for their children is one role that our government should, and must, assume if we, and Rush, expect the need for "welfare" to be eliminated.

Rush has repeatedly referenced generational welfare. Some would argue that living on the "public dole" is a generational, lifestyle choice. After substantial research, real-life experience, and the application of a little deductive reasoning, I have determined that generational welfare is a product of cultural adaptation and role-modeling.

No young girl grows up with aspirations of becoming a single parent living on a few hundred dollars per month, a booklet full of food stamps, in substandard housing, with no adult help to raise her children. That life is not a life worth dreaming about. It is not a life worth aspiring to. Welfare is not a sweepstakes.

Generational welfare comes about when generations of a family grow up in a similar circumstance. A circumstance characterized by fathers who run away and mothers, or grandmothers, who are left to raise children, alone, without resources, without a future, without hope. Children born to families entrenched in generational welfare are children who grow up learning and emulating what they live.

A boy growing up going to bed hungry, or spending months living in a car or a shelter, is bound to learn that a life of poverty, a life without a father to care for him, is simply his reality. His reality becomes his norm. He will then, sadly, likely grow up to continue the cycle. Married and unmarried, mothers in this country are deserted every day.

Children are abandoned by fathers who are capable of producing them, but, seemingly, incapable of attempting to care for them. The majority of these fathers are not incapable. The majority of these fathers just don't care.

Rush speaks of welfare recipients who would rather draw a check than work. I have called, and been an accepted caller, on his radio talk show several times. During my calls, I have tried to explain the fundamental policy that underlies our public assistance system. Because of the brief time allotted for callers, I never got much of a chance to educate Rush on the realities of welfare.

Influential members of the media are powerful forces in public debate. Important public issues of national concern are frequently left at the factual mercy of our media. The biggest, the most far-reaching, have the ability to frame and craft our national opinions. When the national media is mis- or underinformed, we all suffer.

Our welfare recipients are not mothers. Our welfare recipients are not fathers, or grandmothers, or foster parents. Our welfare recipients, the persons for whom the money is paid, are the children. Children who are economically disadvantaged and vulnerable. Children who are without the benefit of an absent parent. Children who are financially neglected.

In his logically presented commentary, Rush expounds on the idea that an entire class of our citizens would prefer to draw a public check than work . . . that a large segment of our population chooses to take public charity over getting up each day and showing up at a job site. Rush needs to know, as does every other person in this country who chimes in on the welfare debate, that welfare payments are for children. Welfare payments are for children who are missing a parent to help take care of them.

Welfare payments were originally, and still are, only supposed to be paid until the parent who walked away is found and forced, under penalty of law, to make child support payments. Child support payments are, by law, intended to replace welfare payments dollar for dollar. When child support is collected, a family's need and eligibility for welfare payments generally end.

Rush and his community of listeners, political compatriots, and fellow like-minded members of the media must understand the following. Ongoing welfare payments are not for adult individuals who are capable of working. Disabled adults may qualify for social security benefits. Nondisabled adults without children cannot qualify for a typical welfare payment. Welfare payments are distributed to the parents of children who are found, via a comprehensive application process, to be without the benefit and support of an absent parent. In addition, the income of the family must be below the amount of a specific cash welfare payment. The payment for a mother and one child might be $278. For a mother and two children, $398. For a family with four children, $475.

A simple look at these numbers unequivocally proves that cash welfare payments are not sufficient to pay for much of anything, let alone fund a lifestyle freely chosen and sought by an adult who just refuses to work. Welfare is not about lazy single mothers. Welfare is about irresponsible, unaccountable fathers. Fathers, married and unmarried, rich and poor, who make babies and decide, for whatever reason, to walk away.

There is both societal and economic value to child care. The societal value of a mother's caring for her own child exists in the basic fact that, generally, no one loves a child like the person who carried and gave birth to that child. The economic value of a mother's caring for her own child has been completely overlooked by the political leadership and media commentators in the welfare debate.

If a mother is not available to care for her child, and if the mother does not have family or friends to provide child care at no cost, she must pay someone else to care for her child. A single parent's working is not without cost. Child care is expensive, not only monetarily. Child care is expensive in that children must be raised by strangers at a developmental and emotional cost that can never be properly assessed.

As a practical matter, a majority of single parents cannot obtain and retain full-time employment because they simply cannot find affordable, safe, reliable child care. A mom working at minimum wage of $5.15 per hour could be, conceivably, charged anywhere from $3.50 to $7.00 per hour for child care. On the low end of child care, she retains only $1.65 per hour of her wages, and that's before taxes. On the high end of child care, she is in the negative by $1.85 per hour. It is ridiculous to assert that a single parent should work to pay child care costs that equal or exceed the pay earned. It is this level of the absurd that has led to the faulty premise that is the foundation of the 1996 welfare reform laws. Work alone is not the answer.

Some formerly wealthy families find themselves on welfare. A father earning a six-figure income can (and some have) leave his family, find a new girlfriend, claim poverty, and cause his lawfully married wife and four legitimate children to be dragged through more than a year of legal proceedings before being forced to pay adequate child support through a court-mandated wage-withholding order. The tactics of fathers, and sometimes mothers, who willfully attempt to avoid supporting their children are not foreign to those who are publicly perceived to be above reproach.

Sadly, the list of delinquent parents includes political representatives, judges, assorted celebrities, members of the clergy, and athletes, who have been elevated to icons in the eyes of some children . . . children just like the ones they refuse to support. Rush can help this cause. He can learn a bit about the realities involved in public assistance programs. He can use his media influence to publicly assert and promote a nationwide "no tolerance" policy with regard to parents, any and all such parents, who walk away from their kids, expecting someone else, or the government, to take care of them.

In addition to spending many hours of many days with Rush, I also spent, and continue to spend, a good deal of time listening to Dr. Laura Schlessinger, another conservative talk show host. The radio stays on in my car as I travel to and from court hearings. The radio stays on in my office as I draft documents and research my cases. Dr. Laura is tough. Dr. Laura is no-nonsense. And, Dr. Laura is right when it comes to the source of America's welfare problem.

Dr. Laura hammers throughout the course of her radio show on the fact that many, far too many, parents in the United States today walk away from their children without consequence. Not only does she refer to this sad circumstance in terms of custodial arrangements, she also refers to it in terms of its economic impact on children. Dr. Laura regularly and adamantly encourages single parents to seek and attempt to obtain the child support their children are lawfully entitled to.

On frequent occasions, I have heard Dr. Laura chastise an ambivalent mom who has called the show asking whether or not she should pursue child support . . . not wanting to "rock the boat" with her child's father. Child support is an entitlement. The law in the United States requires parents to support their children.

Children do not choose to come into this world. We, the adults who bring them here, have no right to neglect, ignore, or mistreat our children. Denying children the support they need is a type of neglect, which should not be tolerated. Clearly, children cannot obtain jobs to support themselves. Why can't the adults grow up and behave like people who have something or someone bigger than themselves to care for?

Dr. Laura is right when she frames every family-related issue she discusses around the needs and best interests of children. When engaging in a national welfare debate, our legislators, community leaders, and media pundits must do the same. Dr. Laura draws a hard line with regard to parents and responsibility. It is past time for our country, society, government, community, and citizens to take the same hard line.

Those that have a national voice must listen to those of us who have lived the lives and the problems and the burdens they pontificate about and profess to understand. Until our country asserts, in a unified voice, that we will no longer tolerate adults who create children and walk away from them, regardless of the reason, the welfare problem will persist. We must, together, make it socially unacceptable for a parent to abandon a child. We must make it culturally uncomfortable for a parent to abandon a child.

We must no longer put up with those who trade their children and families in for new models, or worse, leave those children and families deserted, without the resources necessary to buy food, maintain shelter, and/or seek medical care. Our nation's children are not disposable. There will always be a need for welfare when children are treated with such disregard by so many. And to think that this treatment goes on in a country of enormous resources and affluence. We should all be terribly embarrassed.

Eight

You Have No Rights . . . You're on Welfare

It was always a two-to three-hour process. Waiting in a welfare office was a mind-numbing, stress-inducing, anxiety-producing experience—each and every time. With no money for child care, three toddlers, and a baby on the way, I became inseparable from my children. We all went everywhere together. A crowded, backed-up welfare office was not the place for a hormone-ridden mother-to-be with three young children and forty or so other families, all waiting, it seemed endlessly, for several hours to apply for public assistance. As I scanned the room during each and every appointment, I noticed how different we all looked. Different ages. Different colors. Different languages. Different backgrounds. But, at the same time, we were all the same. We had all been abandoned by either the fathers or the mothers of our children.

I stepped into a welfare office for the first time at the direction of the Fairfax County Juvenile and Domestic Relations Court. Growing up, I had never needed anything. My sister, brother, and I were not spoiled, but, we always had food, clothing, a wonderful place to live, and security. I did not know what a food stamp was, but within ten days, I had my first book of three hundred and some.

The kids and I arrived at the Department of Social Services, located in Reston, Virginia. I took the stroller up to the second floor, parked it carefully in a corner next to an already formed line of strollers, picked up Tricia, took April's hand, and told Phillip to follow along. We took our place at the end of a long queue of mothers and children. The line went out the office door and curled down the hallway. I was certain to be there for hours. At least I had several bottles of juice, a few packs of crackers, and plenty of diapers . . . the few diapers I had left.

We did pretty well during the first hour of our waiting. At one point, a worker from social services walked along the line and took down our names, explaining that although we still needed to wait for our appointments, we could start filling out the forms to get the process started. She handed me a large packet of paperwork that must have been twenty or so pages. With three hungry, squirmy children in tow, my chances of successfully completing that packet that day were slim to none. Thankfully, I was told that I could sign the last page of each document, leave the signed pages with the department, and then wait for a call to setup an appointment.

I drove home feeling that at least I had accomplished something. We pulled up in front of the apartment. The children had fallen asleep on the way home. One by one, I unbuckled their car seats, carried them up the two flights of stairs leading to our apartment, and then drove the car to the rear of the complex. Thankfully, all three slept for several hours after our morning into afternoon adventure. I had a lot of reading to do.

The pamphlets were thick and full of requirements. The task before me seemed impossible. I needed original social security cards for me and each of the children. I hadn't even applied for social security numbers for them, and I had no clue where my card was. I couldn't ask my mother for my card. In addition to the social security cards, I needed to provide original birth certificates for all of us, copies of the kids' pediatric records to prove that they lived with me, copies of my bank records, utility bills, lease, and three household composition forms.

After our last move, I had left most of our papers and documents taped away in cardboard boxes. There was not an abundance of storage room in the apartment, so, it seemed best to leave as much packed away as possible. I had no way of knowing exactly where the birth certificates were. In the interest of time, I reapplied for birth certificates for all of us. Fortunately, I was able to make my requests with the Virginia Department of Vital Records over the telephone. Happy about the relative ease of that phone call, I packed up the bottles, the juice, the crackers, and the kids, put the stroller in the car, and drove to the closest social security office.

It was about a thirty-minute drive to Manassas, Virginia, to apply for social security cards. My sense of accomplishment was short-lived. To my frustration, dismay, and disappointment, individual, original birth certificates were necessary to apply for original social security cards. Not knowing what to do, I grabbed a stack of social security card applications, got the kids back into the car, and headed back home.

It could have been six weeks before the birth certificates arrived. On top of that, it might have been six additional weeks for new social security cards to be processed. Twelve weeks! Twelve weeks would put us beyond the pending August court date. As I drove home from Manassas, an enormous feeling of hopelessness and loneliness came over me. I looked at the sleeping children in my rearview mirror. What had I done? I had married someone who never really cared about me. I had had three children—almost four—with him, and even though I had tried everything I could to fix him and make things right, I knew nothing would ever be right. Sitting at a red light, my eyes filling with tears, I temporarily lost track of where I was. A loud honking car horn interrupted my moment of self-pity and brought me back to reality.

The noise of the horn also woke the sleeping kids. All three began to cry, in a harmony of sorts. That drive home seemed endless. We arrived home, and this time, we all walked from the car's hiding place back to our apartment. Everyone was hungry, and we were almost out of food. I had several boxes of macaroni and cheese left, a few yogurts (banana was their favorite), three cans of orange juice, and two cans of apple juice. I made a quick lunch and put everyone down for a well-deserved nap. Then, I pored over all the social services' paperwork, hoping to find some immediate answers, and help.

I read that the department had up to forty-five days to determine whether I qualified for public assistance. The department had up to thirty days to determine our eligibility for food stamps. Fortunately, in the fine print, I read that if we had fewer than $100 in resources and no income, we could receive an emergency allotment of food stamps within five days. It was an answer to my prayers. I called the department and requested emergency food stamps. Based upon the number in my family, my husband's desertion, and my lack of income, I was approved for an emergency allotment. Two days later, I received a telephone call informing me that I could pick up my food stamp identification card the following Monday morning at a local county building. I was also informed that my food stamps would arrive by certified mail on or after the following Tuesday. The news was good. All I had to do was get through the weekend.

My mom called that weekend and offered to take us out to a local Price Club to do a little shopping. Although I had no money and almost no gas left in the car, I happily accepted her offer, hoping I would get the nerve up to ask for help buying food and diapers. I did my best to be cheerful and tried to act as if everything was fine. My parents were not aware that Eric had still not returned home. They also did not know that another baby was on the way. My mom and I put the car seats carefully in her van. I dressed in baggy clothes, trying to hide my increasing size and expanding waistline.

Off we went to the Price Club. I always enjoyed visiting the Price Club. It is an amazing place with rows of groceries, most in large, economy-size boxes. The kids were always fascinated by the tall shelves and busy atmosphere. This time it was a bit of an escape from the panic of the previous week and the loneliness of my circumstances. I gathered cereal, pasta, laundry detergent, baby powder, diapers, and a number of frozen items in my cart. Thankfully, my mom paid for all of our items, no questions asked. I was grateful, but felt dishonest about accepting her generosity without letting her know the full truth of what was going on.

The remainder of the weekend passed quietly. Under warm, sunny skies, the kids and I spent the rest of Saturday and Sunday taking walks and visiting a small neighborhood playground that was neatly nestled between groups of nearby town homes. It had been more than a week since the awful afternoon outside Kelly's apartment. It had been more than a week since I had seen or heard from Eric. Monday morning arrived quickly. The night before, I remember waking up more often than usual. I watched the clock, and waited. At 8:30 A.M. we could go and get our food stamps. Progress, at last.

I loaded the kids into the car, and, off we went. The government building where I could pick up my food stamp identification card was about twenty-five minutes away. The office for food stamp distribution shared space with the local Fairfax County Police Department. As I turned into the parking lot, Phillip pointed to all of the police cars. One of his favorite toys was a metal police car that lit up and made a siren noise when it was pushed on the floor. After I parked the car, pulled out the stroller, and put everyone in their respective places, we walked up to the police cars for a closer look. Phillip was fascinated to see a life-size version of his toy. For a moment, I forgot why we were there.

Thankfully, and often, my mind was relieved from the stress of our current circumstance with glimpses of pure, unspoiled childhood curiosity. Without the curiosity and innocence of my children's daily living, I would not have survived. We strolled into the office, and, since lines are the way to public benefits, we took our place at the end of the long line and waited for about an hour.

When we reached the front of the line, I presented my driver's license and was promptly handed a paper card. The card was similar to a social security card, but, was yellow and had lots of small print on one side. The stern, lemony smelling clerk warned me that I must have the card with me at all times when using my food stamps. She then took my picture and told me to wait for the photo to develop. We waited just a few more minutes. The photo was done, and we were on our way home. All before noon.

The next two days seemed like an eternity. The morning hours dragged on endlessly. Our wonderful mailman, a Washington Redskins' Hogette on the side, always delivered the mail at the same time—about 3:30 P.M. He was kind and reliable. For two days, no birth certificates, no food stamps. On the third day, I met the mailman at our box. I asked if there was any certified mail for me. When he said there wasn't, I broke down and cried and told him I was waiting for food stamps. He assured me that he would keep watch for my special letter. The next day, he brought the thick, well-taped letter to my door. I quickly signed my name, thanked him, closed the door, and sat down to see, for the first time, what an actual food stamp looked like.

To my surprise, food stamps looked a lot like play money. The ink was dark, the lettering was bold. Food stamps were loud and obvious. Anyone near me in line at a checkout counter would be able to see that I was using food stamps. I put the envelope down, went to the kitchen, and perused the cabinets. They were empty, I had to go food shopping. We had waited for these food stamps. It was time to shop. The kids needed decent food. Macaroni and cheese every day could not be good for them. I decided that after nap time, we would go shopping.

I couldn't risk using the food stamps at out local Giant or Safeway. I didn't want anyone to see me my first time out. So, I packed the kids in the car, stopped at the bank to cash a twenty-five-dollar birthday check I had received from my grandmother for my twenty-sixth birthday, put gas in the car, and, drove to Winchester, Virginia, where Eric's parents lived. Perhaps they would see us using food stamps in their local grocery store. I had called my mother-in-law when Eric left and asked her if she knew where he was. She informed me in harsh tones that she didn't know where he was. When I told her he had left us with nothing, she said, as far as she was concerned, the harder it was for me, the better. I knew she resented me for her having to raise Billy, but, I never thought she would actively help Eric desert and abandon his other children.

The drive to Winchester took almost an hour and a half. The weather was sunny and pleasant, and the ride was peaceful. The children drank their juice and chatted among themselves, as they often did in the car. Most of the time, I couldn't understand exactly what they said to each other. But, I was certain that they had their own way of communicating and that I was not meant to be privy to their conversations. It was a "kid" thing. Maybe even a sibling thing. Even at their young ages, I sensed that the children had developed an incredible bond with each other. Even though I often felt like I was the extent of their world, I was learning that I wasn't everything to them, which was a bit of a relief. To be the only source of everything for a child is difficult, and overwhelming. Fortunately, the kids had each other, and I had them. Even if we were without a husband and father.

I parked at the Food Lion, put the kids in the stroller, and walked toward the store. As I generally did when I wanted to shop for a lot, I connected the stroller to a shopping cart with a long shoelace. I pushed the stroller and guided the shopping cart to follow directly behind. Phillip helped a bit, but then wanted to ride in the shopping cart. With two children in the stroller and one in the cart, we made our way up and down the isles. With food stamps, we could buy any food item, provided it was not hot food from a deli or ready-made, "to go" food. After several weeks of worrying, and wondering how I would get the things my family needed, I was able to choose better items off of the grocery shelf than I was able to before Eric left. The shopping felt like Christmas. Checkout, however, was nothing to celebrate.

I pushed the shopping cart into the checkout aisle and began to unload our groceries. I had been careful to purchase food stamp-acceptable food items only. Having only a few dollars of cash left after my gas purchase, I had to conserve what I had. My diaper supply was running short. With three children in diapers, we went through almost two dozen per day. But, our need for diapers was not on the agenda for that day. Diapers would have to wait.

The kids began to squirm while we waited in line. I had opened a box of saltines as we shopped, but the salt made them thirsty and their patience was running short. So was mine. I fiddled with my books of food stamps, counting the individual coupons to be certain I had enough. I kept the books carefully concealed in my diaper bag until the last possible moment. An elderly couple complaining to each other in soft southern accents stood behind us in line. They seemed nice enough, but, I did not want them to see my food stamps. I was there with three small children, obviously pregnant with number four, using food stamps to pay for our order. What would the couple think? What would anyone think? What would I think if I were watching me and the kids in line? I know what I would think. That is what really hurt the most.

The grocery clerk was very nice. She commented that the children were well-behaved, totaled up our bill, and asked if I had any coupons. Under my breath, I quietly told her that I had food stamps and did not have coupons. She discreetly took the books of food stamps from my hand, checked my signature and picture on my food stamp identification card, took the appropriate number of stamps from the books, and gave me a receipt. After she thanked me for shopping at the store, she whispered to me that even with food stamps, I could use coupons. Also, she explained, I would receive the value of the coupons tendered back in actual cash. This tip was invaluable. It provided me with a way to purchase diapers, baby products, and other nonfood items. From that moment on, I became an avid coupon clipper.

My first experience using food stamps was not as bad as I feared it would be. I made it through without great humiliation and actually picked up information that would help me get the other items I needed for the kids. Driving home, I felt the first sense of actual relief I had felt in months. My car was full of groceries and sleeping children. For at least the remainder of the drive home, I had everything under control. The chaos was quieted, and my worry was quelled. At least for ninety minutes.

I pulled up in front of the apartment, took the kids out of the car one by one and carried them upstairs to their cribs. I placed our grocery bags on the steps in front of the unit, drove the car around to its hiding place, and practically ran back to get the groceries in the apartment. I made a great dinner that night of boneless chicken breasts, salad with turkey and several types of shredded cheese, and soft, sweet Hawaiian bread. The kids loved Hawaiian bread. It was a good night, and the next few days would be better.

The following day, our birth certificates arrived in the mail. I immediately drove back to the social security office, applied for cards for all of us, received receipts for our applications, and returned to Fairfax County Social Services. It was a good moment when I was finally able to turn over the documentation the county required to process my request for public assistance. I was told I would have an answer by the end of the month. I went back home, and waited.

In an effort to "earn" enough money to buy diapers and nonfood items, I clipped coupons aggressively. Based upon what the grocery clerk told me, I knew I could accumulate cash when using my food stamps by off-setting some of the food stamp costs with in-store coupons. I was thankful for this creative alternative. Eric was certainly not forthcoming with any money. Our court date was more than a month away, and I had not yet been approved for public assistance. But with coupons and ingenuity, we would have diapers.

By the end of June 1990, I received a letter of approval for public assistance, ongoing food stamps, and medicaid. We would have food, $378 per month in cash assistance, and medical coverage. We also, however, had an eviction notice and needed to be out of the apartment by the end of July. With no job, no income other than welfare, and three small children and one on the way, where would we go? We were going to be homeless, I just knew it. I couldn't ask to move in with my mom and dad. I had chosen Eric. I had created the situation, and now I had to deal with it. I had to find a place. Fast.

I scoured through local newspapers searching for a privately owned unit to rent. With my dubious income and lack of employment, I would never survive a commercial rental application process. I had to find a private owner who could meet me, realize that I would take good care of his or her property, and be willing to give me and the kids a chance. I was fortunate to find just such a place, and just such owners. It was a two-level townhouse in Centreville. The rent was $750 per month—almost double the public assistance payment. Desperate, I called my sister. She graciously agreed to cosign the lease with me and helped me to cover the first month's rent and security deposit. In addition, the county's department of social services helped us with security deposits for our utilities. We had a place. We just needed a way to move.

The house was tiny, but nice. There was a small backyard of grass, and the front of the home was skirted by sidewalks. It was a perfect place for tricycle and Big Wheel riding. I was happy and hopeful that this house would be a good home for us. Fairfax County contracted with Campbell Moving Company for moves related to evictions and homeless families. Campbell helped me to move all of my large items, including beds, cribs, the couch, and dressers. I had to deal with the smaller items myself. Throughout the moving process I heard nothing from Eric, even though he knew we were being evicted by August 1 and that I had no money. He did not attempt to call or to help.

Finally, our day in court was upon us. We appeared before the Honorable Arnold P. Kassabian. I did not have an attorney, but the judge helped me get through that first hearing. He read the petitions I had filed. First, the judge addressed the custody petitions. Per the suggestion of Mr. Rich at the intake department, I had requested sole physical and legal custody of the children, with supervised visitation at my discretion. Eric failed to object. The order was entered. That was it, and it stands to this day.

Next, was the matter of support. As a public assistance recipient, I had no lawful right to receive financial support directly from Eric. Thankfully, no one from the Division of Child Support Enforcement showed up for our hearing. Because no one was there, Judge Kassabian listened to my evidence and entered orders for both child and spousal support. We were to receive child support in the amount of $675 per month. I was also to receive spousal support in the amount of $203 per month. It was not a lot of money. But, together, the two support awards would be enough to pay the rent. I thanked the judge and left the courthouse. Eric followed me. He asked why I was doing "this." I was at a loss for words. After being left with nothing, what did he expect me to do? What does any deserting parent expect the other parent to do?

September 1 came quickly, and no support was forthcoming. I was one month away from my due date. I called the telephone number I had been given for Fairfax County's Division of Child Support Enforcement. After being put through a myriad of voice menus, told that all representatives were busy, and asked to hold, I held for more than an hour. After waiting more than an hour, my connection was arbitrarily lost. It took a full week of tries before I reached an actual person. During the call I was frustrated and distraught, and the attitude of the person on the other end of the line did nothing to alleviate my aggravation.

The customer service representative was blatantly rude and condescending toward me on the telephone. I calmly explained that I had a court order for child and spousal support, that I was supposed to receive $878 per month on the first of every month, that my rent of $750 was overdue, and that I had not received my money. After letting out a sigh of obvious disgust, she informed that support payments were not technically "overdue" until the payments were a full thirty days late.

She went on to ask me for my social security number so she could pull up my child support account on her computer screen. "Oh," she remarked. I lost my patience, asked for her supervisor, and told her that after a week of trying to get some answers, I had a right to know what was going on with my support case. She then said, "You have no rights. You get welfare. As long as the state is taking care of your kids, you have no rights. As long as you cash your check, you have no rights." Her words reached through the telephone line and hit me in the stomach. I hung up the phone. I felt sick, ran to the bathroom, and threw up.

Nine

Don't You Believe in Birth Control?

I counted the days between my monthly receipt of that certified mail. There never seemed to be enough stamps to cover all the formula and all the juice and all the Cheerios I needed to feed three small children. When the mailman delivered that certified letter containing our monthly allotment of food stamps, life was a little bit better—at least for that day, provided I could get uneventfully through my shopping trip.

The month of September 1990 was rough. Eric didn't pay child or spousal support. He moved into a town home in Reston with two women he met while working at a Texaco station in Vienna, Virginia. Of course, he gave them his usual sob story. I was the horrible, nagging wife who took all of his money. He was the poor, suffering, mistreated husband. And, he did not tell them how many children we had. With a monthly income of $378 welfare only, I obviously couldn't afford to stay in the town house I had rented. My hope to receive enough support to pay the rent was fading fast. I had to come up with an alternative, or we really would be homeless.

Out of desperation, I called Eric and begged him to help us. His response to my plea was to put a block on my telephone number so I could not reach him. Trying to appeal to his sense of obligation was neither a reasonable nor a wise use of time and energy. Even though it was excruciatingly obvious that Eric did not care about me or the kids, I still had some hope—somewhere, deep-down, where common sense did not exist.

I called Fairfax County's Information and Referral Hotline, hoping to find a resource that could point me toward housing I could afford. Again, the wait on the telephone was long, but the information I received was well worth the wait. A polite call screener took general information from me. She asked for my name, the names of the children, our address, our monthly income, our birthdates, my monthly expenses, and a brief description of why we were in the fix we were in. Some of the questions were intrusive, but, in light of the fact I was seeking financial and/or other help for my family in a difficult circumstance, I would answer whatever questions necessary. My kids came first. My pride was no longer a consideration.

I was referred to an organization in Vienna, Virginia, called Our Daily Bread. Our Daily Bread helped families who were homeless and families who were in jeopardy of becoming homeless by providing emergency assistance with rent and security deposit funds. The worker from the referral service called Our Daily Bread on my behalf and paved the way for us to receive assistance with our rent so that we could have another month to either receive our support or find alternative housing. Another month of rent coverage would get us past the due date for the baby. That was an enormous relief for me.

The pregnancy had been stress-filled from the start. I was not able to obtain prenatal care until my seventh month, because of the long process involved in applying for medicaid. Having a fourth baby in the midst of a nonexistent marriage was not practical. It certainly was not planned. Eric and I hardly spoke to or saw each other after he was released from Dominion Hospital in 1989. However, I had made vows, and I was determined to keep my commitment. I never breached my commitment. If Eric wanted a divorce, he could seek one. That was my outlook on the situation. I was not a quitter. My marriage to Eric had probably saved me from chronic, if not fatal, anorexia. I had to try to save the marriage. It did not make sense. It frustrated my family. It puzzled my social workers. But, it was my life and the life I had created for my kids. It was my responsibility to take care of my children, no matter what.

After receiving confirmation that help was coming with the rent, to celebrate, I gathered the kids, we packed up the car and went grocery shopping. After several months of using food stamps,

I had grown accustomed to the dubious looks I sometimes received and became numb to most offensive remarks I heard from people in the line behind me. On this particular day, I chose to visit our local Super Fresh. I had a large collection of coupons to use and hoped to get newborn diapers in addition to those I needed for Phillip, April, and Tricia.

We strolled around the store and gathered our usual staples of cereal, hot dogs, yogurt, and macaroni and cheese. I piled several bags of diapers on top of the stroller, added some baby powder, laundry detergent, and baby shampoo and proceeded to the check-out. The gentleman at the register scanned our items and abruptly stated the total due. I handed him my food stamp books. He called out to another store employee that he had "food stamps on isle 4" and needed assistance. With this, the line behind me began to grow longer and the faces of other patrons grew dark with frustration. The clerk then informed me that I owed an additional $15 and some cents. I offered him my coupons, knowing that the total value of the coupons exceeded $15 and some cents. The worker harshly responded that "people with food stamps aren't allowed to use coupons," and, that "you can't make money off of food stamps." I stood in disbelief. I never expected his attitude or his harsh treatment of me. I was just about nine months pregnant with three small children and several booklets of food stamps. After he removed the diapers and detergent and powder and shampoo from my already packed paper bags, he turned to me and asked, "Don't you believe in birth control?" I couldn't even look at him. I gathered our food, looked at the floor, and walked out.

Several days later, I had an obstetrician appointment. I arranged for a neighbor to watch the kids so I could have an ultrasound examination. I usually had to bring all of the children to any doctor's appointments any of us had. We were a unit. I could not afford a baby-sitter. I had to reserve asking friends for favors for emergency situations only. I didn't want to take advantage of the people that stood behind me. One day, I might really need someone's help so, I didn't want to ask for too much.

I drove out to Annandale for my appointment. To my frustration and disappointment, the doctor never showed up. The practice

I went to was the only practice I could find in Northern Virginia that accepted medicaid. With my first three children, I had had a wonderful, private obstetrician. With baby number four and no health insurance, I had no choice but to go to any doctor that would take my medicaid card. I did not feel safe. I did not think that my baby would get adequate care, and I was right. I was grateful to have medical care, but, after my experience with military medical care and my miscarriage in Germany, I was fearful of poor care that might cause a difficult situation to be made worse.

It was another week before my appointment could be rescheduled. Again, I made arrangements for the kids. Again, the doctor did not show up. This time, however, a nurse agreed to perform the ultrasound anyway. I was close to my due date. The baby's heart rate seemed elevated, and, the nurse, I could tell, sensed my growing anger. As a general rule, I didn't subscribe to stereotyping, however, in this case, it was clear that the medical care I obtained with medical assistance was not of the same quality it would have been with a doctor of my own choosing. Again, I was angry with Eric. He had lost our decent health insurance and our opportunity to have good, quality medical care. He had put the kids and me in a detrimental, and perhaps even harmful, situation and didn't give it a second thought.

My sister, Patti, agreed to be at the hospital with me for the delivery. My emotions regarding Eric were unstable, uncertain, and indiscernible. I loved him. I hated him. I never wanted to see him again. I did not want him to miss the baby's birth. He should be there to bond with the baby. He did not care, so why would it matter if he was there or not? I was so confused. My life was in turmoil. My hormones were running high, and my hope for a future family life with my husband was as low as it could be.

Patti was a stabilizing force for me during the rough time in 1990. She helped me find a home, helped me keep a home, helped me take care of the kids, and postponed her move to Los Angeles, California, to begin her new job as an associate in a huge, high-caliber law firm so that she could help me through the delivery. I was, and am, very fortunate to have a sister like Patti. My children could not have a better aunt. I do not know how I would have gotten through that difficult year without her.

Ten

Dollars and Sense

Welfare is not a sweeptakes. Welfare emerged from President Eisenhower's 1953 creation of the U.S. Department of Health, Education, and Welfare, now known as the U.S. Department of Health and Human Services. Welfare began as an entitlement program designed to protect children from being left with no source of support after being abandoned by a parent.

Welfare is money for children and their needs. It is not for their parents. It is not a "free ride," nor is it profitable to live on welfare. To qualify for welfare, an applicant must generally be the biological parent of an abandoned child or children, must have no steady source of income, must have no real assets to speak of, and must not own a vehicle with significant value.

To qualify for welfare, children must be deserted and parents must be destitute. Common sense dictates that the way of welfare is no way to live. I know these things because I lived these things. I know these things because I have argued with and debated people who loudly profess to "know" the welfare system without ever having lived it.

Welfare is not about the worn, dirty man sitting on a median strip holding a torn piece of cardboard asking for spare change. Welfare is not about the elderly, unshaven man seen lying on the sidewalk, propped up against a brick wall, holding a paper bag molded by his leathery hand into the shape of a booze bottle. Welfare is not about the alleged African American mother living in public housing in downtown Chicago with twelve children with thirteen possible fathers. Welfare is about attempting to protect children. That's it. If welfare is going to be "reformed," welfare must first be understood.

The economic reality of having and raising a child is that children are expensive. Children require support sufficient to provide shelter, food, clothing, heat, shoes, toiletries, school supplies, and everything else they need to grow, develop, and mature. Certainly, even a judgmental mind can discern that a cash welfare payment of two-hundred and fifty plus dollars per month is not sufficient to meet the daily needs of a child.

From Orlando, Florida, to Fairfax, Virginia, to Warwick, Rhode Island, a simple loaf of supermarket bread can cost anywhere from fifty cents to two dollars. A gallon of milk, anywhere from two dollars and fifty cents to four dollars and fifty cents. A two-liter bottle of soda, anywhere from sixty-nine cents to two dollars and nineteen cents. The cost of food continues to increase. As children grow, the cost of feeding them increases, also.

New mothers are encouraged to nurse their babies. Not only "welfare" moms who access public health clinics and medicaid services, but every mother is encouraged to breast feed her baby because doing so is considered by most pediatric professionals to be the most nourishing way to feed a baby. Many mothers who find themselves alone to have and care for their babies do not have the resources to buy enough food to nourish themselves properly during pregnancy or during the time they might nurse their babies.

In addition to poor nutrition on the part of mothers, poor nutrition is frequently found among children of single mothers who have limited financial resources. The U.S. Department of Agriculture's food stamp programs are available to assist families—who meet certain qualifications—who need help getting food. However, general food stamp allotments are often not sufficient to meet the nutritional needs of expecting moms, new babies, and children under six, particularly children with existing nutritional deficiencies.

In an attempt to address the special nutritional needs of poor women and young children, the federal government established the Women's, Infants', and Children's Nutritional Program, commonly referred to as WIC. To qualify for assistance under the WIC program, a family must be of low or no income, must include an expectant mother, an infant, and/or a child under six years of age. Some families with children over the age of six might qualify for the program provided the children are shown to have specific nutritional deficiencies or needs.

The WIC program issues individual checks to families for the purchase of certain food items that fall under the purview of the program and satisfy USDA requirements with regard to nutritional value. The checks are payable for a specified amount for the limited purchase of specified food. The checks are not payable to the family. The payee of the checks becomes the grocery store or supermarket that accepts the checks as payment for items such as whole milk, 2% milk, 1% milk, (skim milk is not allowed); baby formula; baby food packaged in jars; baby juice packaged in jars or bottles; certain cereals, including Cheerios, Raisin Bran, Wheaties, and other whole grain cereals; eggs; whole chunks of cheese; real fruit juices; and other limited dairy products.

The application process required for the WIC program is complicated and requires a family to participate in a series of appointments at a public health clinic. The first step includes a financial screening and verification of household income and composition. This screening is comprehensive and requires that families produce documentation of all sources of income, general expenses such as rent, utilities, and extraordinary medical expenses, household composition, and proof of any and all assistance received by the family.

Once a family qualifies financially for the program, the individual members of the family are screened for weight, lead exposure, and blood chemistry. In a case involving a child over the age of six, the department must find that a child is anemic or in some other way nutritionally impaired if that child is to qualify for WIC benefits. Categorically, most children and pregnant/lactating women of low or no income qualify for WIC benefits. After a family is certified through the screening process, the head of household, usually a single mother, receives an additional appointment at the clinic for the disbursement and receipt of her WIC checks.

When I was expecting my last daughter, I came to the realization that our food stamp allotment was not sufficient to cover the amount of juice and milk and cereal that my three young children needed each month. We received approximately three hundred dollars per month in food stamps. I was frugal and careful with the allotment. Even so, it was never enough during the last days of each month.

At the urging of my social worker, I applied to the WIC program. I called to make an appointment at the local health clinic and felt embarrassed and humiliated when I was questioned about my personal life and my level of education in the process of simply scheduling an appointment. We waited three weeks for our first appointment.

I bundled up the kids and drove to the clinic. We carried in a bag of things to do and crackers and juice. The wait was long and frustrating—more than four hours. When our name and number were called, we proceeded into a small examination room. We were all weighed, the children were measured. The nurse inquired as to the health history of each of us, and she filled out numerous forms with our information. All three of the children were required to have their blood screened for lead and anemia.

Although I was appreciative of the opportunity to receive extra help with our need for food, I became upset, and even angry, as the public health nurse attempted to draw blood from my three small, frightened children. The kids screamed in fear when she walked into the room with three hypodermic needles. It had been my understanding that only a fingertip test was necessary, but the nurse said that a regular blood draw was required from each of the children named in the application.

The nurse did a terrible job. She was impatient, she was unkind and held the kids roughly as she tried to stick them with the needles. She reprimanded me, saying that I needed to control the children so that she could get the blood drawn. Tears welled in my eyes during that awful afternoon. I had subjected my children to a horrible experience because I didn't have enough money to feed them, and because their dad didn't care enough to help me feed them.

We eventually qualified for WIC, and I was invited back to the clinic to pick up the WIC checks. Using WIC checks is far more conspicuous than using food stamps. Using WIC checks is also cumbersome for grocery store cashiers, because all items purchased must be separated and each check covers payment for only certain items. A grocery order including three gallons of milk, two cartons of eggs, twelve jars of baby food, two boxes of cereal, several bricks of cheese, and four bottles of juice could conceivably require a cashier to check out six, separate orders. Six separate receipts. Six separate transactions. One frustrated cashier, and a line full of unhappy customers.

I applied for, and received, WIC one time. The embarrassment I experienced while trying to use the WIC checks in my local grocery store was more than I could bear. When my last daughter was an infant, following a period of her hospitalization, I needed to purchase formula for a period of time while she recuperated.

However, waiting in line while a cashier sorted through each and every item, while my three toddlers and new infant grew hungry and increasingly impatient, coupled with my memory of the terrible time we had experienced during the health screening process, made me determined never to seek WIC benefits again. Many grocery stores, formerly required to honor WIC checks, now have the option of whether or not to accept such checks. Many of those stores now refuse WIC checks because of the time and paperwork involved in the facilitation of the program.

Finding food sufficient to feed one's family is one of the greatest challenges for a single parent. Thankfully, all across our nation, thousands of churches and community organizations have gathered resources and established food banks, food closets, and food pantries. At first thought, the idea of visiting a food bank might be uncomfortable. But, for single moms with no food for their children, a food bank is a tremendous blessing. Many food closets and pantries have become increasingly creative in their programs, funding sources, and methods of food distribution.

A food pantry that I frequented for several years in the Northern Virginia area was set up in a small building and looked similar to the inside of a friendly neighborhood mom-and-pop grocery store. The pantry was open several afternoons each week, was available by appointment only, and could be accessed by any person in need, provided he or she had some type of identification to present. I called the pantry, made an appointment, and took my children one afternoon for our first visit.

I was a bit apprehensive about going to a neighborhood pantry and was concerned that I might run into someone I knew. To my relief and surprise, the experience was very good. My children and I "shopped" happily for an hour, picking up name-brand macaroni and cheese, yogurt, seedless green grapes, and a few bakery treats that were neatly stacked on large bakery trays. That day, we all went home happy. That night, we all ate well.

Quality health care is difficult for many single parents to obtain. The federal government's medical assistance program, entitled Medicaid, was developed to assist the poorest families in our nation with access to basic medical care. Pregnant women, children under the age of six, and families receiving public assistance cash grants are categorically eligible for medicaid. Medicaid may be used in a manner similar to private insurance; however, the services available under medicaid coverage are generally limited and provided by practitioners who specifically register with the government as medicaid providers.

Families with medicaid coverage can obtain limited medical services with no out-of-pocket cost. In addition, prescription medications will be provided to most families at no out-of-pocket cost. The pool of medicaid providers a family has to choose from is limited. Although medicaid funds will be paid to doctors who serve medicaid patients, those funds are limited to what the government considers a usual and customary fee. Doctors who participate in the medicaid program must write off a certain amount of fees for each patient treated, because medicaid funds will not cover most private practitioners' standard, full fees for service.

I was a medicaid patient when I delivered my last daughter. As a medicaid recipient in 1990, I could find only one obstetrician in Northern Virginia who would accept me as a patient. I could not get an initial appointment with the doctor until I was in my seventh month. Although I was not personally comfortable with the doctor (I had had a wonderful, female obstetrician deliver my first three children), I was thankful to have at least some prenatal care.

After having had three babies and one miscarriage, I knew how vital prenatal care is to the good health of a baby. After having a private obstetrician, I knew what good, quality care was and how much it cost. Having no income other than a welfare grant of three hundred and some dollars, I was grateful to have a doctor to deliver my baby.

As a medicaid patient, I was a low priority. Several times, I went to the doctor's office, waited an hour or so, and was turned away because the doctor was not available. But, as a medicaid patient and a mom with no other options, I did what I had to do. When the time came for my delivery, I had a few minor difficulties. My water broke, but the doctor would not believe me. When I checked in to the hospital, I had to wait several hours for a room. While I was in labor, several residents and small groups of medical students came into my room and performed tests that, I did not know until later, were purely instructional and had no bearing on my delivery. To my dismay, I learned that the rights of a medicaid patient are different from the rights of a "regular," paying patient. The hospital was entitled to use my case for teaching purposes. There was not much I could do about it. I had no other option.

For a single parent with small children, safety can be a nagging concern. When one adult has to be all things to a helpless child, that adult needs access to assistance in times of trouble. Access to a telephone during an emergency is a necessity for families with young children. Many families living on public assistance cannot afford regular telephone service, and thus, live without the safety net 911 provides. Welfare payments are minimal and do not cover all basic necessities and are not sufficient to pay for telephones and telephone service. To that end, local telephone companies in various jurisdictions offer low-rate, basic telephone service to medicaid families. For approximately three dollars per month, some phone companies will provide limited, local service to families receiving medicaid. Welfare payments are not intended to take care of all needs of a family. The parent in the home, and, the parent out of the home, are, technically, charged with taking care of the needs of their family.

Diapers are a necessity for every family with infants or toddlers. As a practical matter, a newborn can go through up to fifteen diapers each day. A toddler, especially a potty-training toddler, might use ten. A standard pack of brand-name diapers generally runs approximately fourteen dollars for twenty-eight to forty-eight diapers, depending on the size of diaper purchased. A single mom with two children, ages six months and three years, could conceivably spend two hundred and ninety-four dollars each month for diapers alone.

If that same mom receives a welfare payment of three hundred and seventy-eight dollars per month, she will be left with eighty-four dollars to cover her rent, household supplies, utilities, and any food items that her food stamp allotment might not cover. Clearly, a single parent with several young children cannot survive on "welfare" alone. How can any reasonable person fairly allege that this type of lifestyle is something that single mothers aspire to?

Obtaining affordable housing is, and has always been, the greatest obstacle to a family's self-sufficiency. Without a place to live, single mothers—single parents—and their children seek refuge under bridges, in shelters, old motels, flophouses, tents, cars, and in homes over-occupied by large, extended families. Public perception seems to be that "free" housing is handed to "welfare mothers." Housing, free or otherwise, is never "handed" to anyone involved in federal housing assistance.

The federal government's Department of Housing and Urban Development oversees government-assisted housing programs across the country. Under the Section 8 program, a federal program of housing subsidies set forth in the United States Code, families can obtain and rent private housing with the help of a payment voucher. The payment voucher traditionally covers a portion of the rent sufficient to limit a family's contribution to approximately 30 percent.

The federal government also provides public housing units—units that are established pursuant to the United States Code and are available to qualified, low or no income persons seeking a place to live. Public housing units are owned and operated by the government. Both Section 8 properties and public housing units are generally perceived by the public to be undesirable and illicit, and there is "not in my backyard" attitude from communities where such housing exists. Over 70 percent of families living in assisted housing units are headed by single mothers. Without assisted housing, these families would be in shelters, motels, tents, or worse.

Unfortunately, people often categorize families living in assisted housing as being undesirable, drug involved, delinquent, and lazy. The reality of assisted housing is that thousands of families sit on waiting lists for two to five years, waiting for a chance to be screened for housing assistance. Families must apply, document their finances, present references, earn some type of income unless disabled, and must establish a favorable history as a tenant with a prior landlord before being allowed to rent under a subsidized program.

The application process for housing assistance is not physically invasive, as is the WIC program. However, the process for housing assistance triggers a strict level of scrutiny over a family, their household composition, their activities, their finances, and their housekeeping skills. I am not advocating that the process should be lax or without the scrutiny that exists. As a resident myself, I am thankful for the scrutiny. I am simply frustrated that the poor public perception of housing programs in the United States today serves as an insurmountable barrier to the growth of needed, affordable, safe housing for our most fragile families.

The housing assistance, Section 8 voucher I received in 1991 has enabled me to have a safe, reliable, affordable home for my children. My housing assistance has enabled me to go to graduate school and law school, to—after three tries—pass the Virginia bar exam, obtain and retain a position as a legal aid attorney, and has helped my family and me move from public assistance to self-sufficiency. It has taken almost twelve years, and, I am very thankful.

Every family needs water, heat, and electricity to survive. Water, heat, and electricity can be, and often are, very expensive services to obtain. For a single mother on welfare, heat is often a luxury, and air-conditioning is unheard of. As with telephone service, welfare payments are neither intended nor sufficient to cover the monthly costs of utilities for a family.

Some state social services departments provide limited assistance with overdue utility bills. Generally, an applicant must seek aid with a cutoff or disconnection notice in hand. The Salvation Army also provides limited assistance with overdue utility bills, as do many church groups and nonprofit organizations.

During the course of my three years as a welfare recipient, and my subsequent years living with a very low income, at one time or another, our lights, our heat, our water, our telephone have all been disconnected. At one point, my large, green trash bin was repossessed. I have been to the Salvation Army for help. I have asked local church groups to help me so that my kids could have lights at night. I qualified several times for fuel assistance through Virginia's program for its poorest citizens.

I have accessed all these resources, not willingly, but out of need. Bills are black and white statements of what it takes, what it costs, to keep services going. When a deserted family struggles to survive on a welfare check and a hope that child support might one day appear in the mailbox, nothing is black and white. When a deserted family struggles to survive on a welfare check and hope, every day is a fuzzy blur of wondering how the rent will be paid, how the lights will be kept on, and how the food will be purchased.

For most of us, economic survival is a matter of dollars and cents. For single mothers, deserted families, and children in need, economic survival is a matter of dollars and sense.

Eleven

A Lonely Ride

I made a deal with God. I knew my water had broken several days ago. This was my fourth baby, and I knew that something was just not right. Labor was not progressing. I ran up and down the hills outside of the hospital in an effort to get things moving, but, to no avail. I would have to have another induction. The first three hadn't been too bad, but this time, I was a medicaid patient, and as such, I was "open season" for resident practice and medical student observation. The baby's heart monitor registered 210, 220, 230, 260. It was way too high. I was concerned, so I buzzed a nurse, but a resident assured me that "the equipment was not always accurate." Everything was alright, he said—but, it wasn't.

I had a craving for Junior Mints, and Patti offered to go buy some for me at the hospital gift shop. It was a Sunday afternoon, and I was debating whether or not to call Eric and tell him that the baby was coming. After talking it over with Patti, I decided to call him. He had been there when the other kids were born. Knowing that he didn't feel responsible for the children he had seen come into the world, I was fearful that if he wasn't there when the newest baby was born, he would feel even less attached to her. Although Eric had a habit of telling his acquaintances that he questioned the paternity of the baby, he never questioned paternity while he was in court or with me.

Several hours later, labor was still not progressing, and Eric arrived at the hospital. At 6:00 P.M., the resident on duty told me that the doctor in charge had written the order for my labor to be induced. Having had three prior inductions, I knew, generally, what to expect. Once an epidural anesthetic was begun, induced labor was manageable. But, without a good anesthetic, induced labor has the effect of being run over by a train. When induced labor hits, it hits hard. Emotionally, this time, I was not ready to handle another baby. I was so worried about finances, and food, and court, and keeping a roof over our heads. Inside, I felt like I was falling apart. Outside, I had to be strong. With four children under the age of four and a life that, for all intents and purposes, was a complete mess, I had to live above my problems. I had to rise above the problems, reach inside for strength, ask God for lots of help, and be sincerely appreciative and grateful for my family members and true friends.

Once the nurse began the Pitocin drip for the induction, I was connected to a standard fetal monitor. Again, as had been the case in the doctor's office several weeks earlier, the baby's heart rate was registering 210, 220, 230, and 260. Again, I expressed my concern and was assured that the equipment was not always accurate. But, this time, I did not accept the nurse's answer, and instead I asked for the practice's on-call doctor. I was informed that he was on his way to the hospital and would arrive shortly. When the doctor arrived, I told him my concerns, then began to feel very sick to my stomach. I didn't know if it was caused by the labor or the Junior Mints. My sister was certain the Junior Mints were at fault.

While conducting a standard labor check, the doctor's face looked a bit anxious. He asked the nurse to send for a social worker. Upon hearing that, I panicked. The doctor explained that the baby had turned "sunny-side up," and that a cesarean section might be needed to deliver her, because she was in a position not conducive to a normal delivery. With his words, fear filled my mind and my heart began to race. There was no way I could have a c-section. Not with four small children to care for alone.

Patti tried to assure me that everything would be OK. Although Eric said that he would help me, I knew that help would never come. There was no way I could have major surgery and be able to recover and take proper care of the kids on my own. I knew that. That was my reality. I prayed fast, and I prayed hard. I often wondered what

God thought of the choices I had made—marrying someone who was no more responsible than an average, hormone-ridden high school teenage boy, having four children with him, one after he had already left us on numerous occasions. What had I been thinking? Where was my common sense? How could I make a deal with God when my choices had been so poor? I was in a horrible dilemma, but I prayed anyway. I had a feeling God would hear me and help me. And he did. Before the doctor sent the nurse to get a room set up for a cesarean section, I asked him to check the baby's position one more time. Begrudgingly he consented to my request. To his amazement, the baby had turned. He implored me to push fast, before she could turn back out of position. Her heart rate continued to be high, but at 8:03 P.M. three minutes after the conclusion of an episode of *Life Goes On,* Megan Sandra Cave was born. Patti and Eric took her to the nursery for the usual bath, measurements, and new-baby cleanup procedures. I was exhausted, relieved, and promised to never be in such a position ever again.

The next evening, Patti, my mom, and the rest of the children came to visit us. Phillip, April, and Tricia were fascinated with baby Megan. I enjoyed my time in the hospital. I kept Megan with me and realized that that time in the hospital was likely the only time I would have alone with any of my children. It was precious time that I will always treasure. Patti had been so helpful and supportive. She had always been the practical one. She tried to talk sense into me throughout the course of my rocky marriage, but, instead of judging me, she listened to me and put up with me. And, she did anything and everything she could for the kids.

That night, Patti and I had to say good-bye. She was off to her new job in Los Angeles. I knew that four small children and I would not be flying to California anytime soon, so I held on to her promise to come home for a visit at Thanksgiving. Even though Patti had not always lived nearby, she had always been there for us. It was so hard to see her go. I knew that once she moved to Los Angeles, she would not likely return to Virginia to live.

The day after I left the hospital, my friend Ruby, who was a student in a class I taught in Reston, Virginia, came to visit with her four-month-old baby, Joshua. It was comforting to have another adult in the house. Ruby had a Subaru station wagon, which had room for five car seats, so we traveled around Northern Virginia in her car while she visited. On the second day of Ruby's visit, she offered to take us all out to the grocery store. I showed Ruby my food stamps and filled her in on some of the troubles I faced using them in local stores. Eric had yet to pay his court-ordered support. Upon hearing that, Ruby suggested that she and I and all five of the kids pay him a visit at the grocery store where he worked. She had no problem asking him for the support. She knew how much it was needed.

Ruby liked to use lists and schedules, so she prepared a shopping list. I was more of a take-things-as-they-come kind of person; I never shopped with a list. Our entourage made its way up and down the isles of the Weis Market, the fourth or fifth grocery store Eric had worked at. Each time a wage-withholding order was delivered to an employer, Eric moved on to another job. After filling our baskets with the items on the list, we checked out, and I paid for the order with my food stamps. Ruby and I both thought that, Eric would surely be embarrassed for his wife, three toddlers, and newborn baby to have to use food stamps in the store where he worked. But, if he was, it wasn't evident. Eric wasn't bothered one bit by the fact that his family had to use food stamps. In fact, he seemed relieved to not have to worry about feeding the kids. With food stamps, why worry?

Eric was restocking shelves near the front of the store, when we approached him. The kids shouted, "Hi Daddy!" Ruby said hello. I said nothing. Ruby told Eric that we were there to pick up the support money, but Eric told her that he didn't have any money, because he had used it for his rent and car payment. There we were. Megan was six days old. We waited in the store for two hours. Ruby told him that we wouldn't leave until he gave us the money, but he just ignored us. Finally, the manager asked us to leave. Feeling rejected and extremely sad and disappointed, I cried, and Ruby gave me some words of encouragement and gathered the kids together. We walked out to the Subaru, put the groceries in the rear of the car, and drove back to the house.

That night, Megan cried for several hours. I couldn't figure out why she was crying. She didn't have colic, and her appetite seemed normal. She didn't have a fever. I walked her, rocked her, bounced her, fed her. Even Ruby took a turn trying to calm her. Our efforts went on for a couple of hours, until, finally, at about 10:00 P.M., Megan fell asleep. The next evening, her crying began again, and she cried again until about 10:00 P.M. This time, however, she had a fever, and this time, when her crying stopped, she fell asleep and wouldn't wake up. I was terrified. Ruby was calm and immediately called, Dr. Schwartz, our pediatrician. He was an excellent doctor. I had gone to him as a child and trusted him implicitly.

After Dr. Schwartz heard the description of Megan's symptoms, he asked a few more questions and calmly told us he was calling 911 for an ambulance. Ruby suggested that I get a few things together. She called my mom, and when the ambulance arrived, she followed us out, helped us get in, and promised to take care of the other kids. She was amazing. I don't know what I would have done without her.

The paramedics tried to keep me calm. One technician tried to wake Megan up. When she couldn't wake her, she asked the driver to step up the speed. It felt like I was in a dream. I had no idea what could be wrong. The EMTs told me to remain calm, but there was no way I could. The drive to the hospital seemed like an eternity. When we pulled in front of the emergency room entrance, a group of doctors came out and took Megan into a trauma room. I had to wait in the hallway. It was frightening to stand outside of the trauma room watching staff members rush in and out. They tested her blood, took her temperature, and performed a spinal tap. They poked her and tested her, and finally an IV had to be put in the heal of her foot. No immediate answer as to what was happening to Megan was forthcoming.

Finally, after I had waited more than an hour, the doctor came to see me. He informed me that Megan was stable. They had been able to wake her up, and she had taken some formula. He went on to say that they hadn't been able to determine what was causing the crying and the periods of deep sleep, but, they were able to see that her heart rate was running very high. He said the periods of high heart rate coincided with the intense crying episodes, implying that the two factors were related. He admitted Megan into the pediatric wing of the hospital. My mom arrived later and agreed to take care of Phillip and April. Ruby would stay at my house with Tricia and Joshua. Everyone would be taken care of, so that I could stay at the hospital with Megan. I was thankful for this help during the emergency. I don't know how I would have made it through without Ruby and my mother.

Megan had to stay in the hospital for four days. An IV remained connected to her foot, making it difficult to hold her, and her hospital crib looked more like a plastic bubble than a baby's bassinet. Fortunately, with Ruby at my house with Joshua and Tricia, and my mom keeping April and Phillip, I was able to stay at the hospital every night and most of every day. The doctors could not pinpoint what was causing Megan's often erratic heart rate. When Megan's fever was under control and her blood tested free of bacteria, the doctors determined that we could go home. It was a relief—for all of us. April and Phillip wanted to go home, and Tricia missed the rest of us. Ruby needed to return to her home and her husband, Tim. It had been a long and difficult week. I hoped for a return to some sort of normalcy.

But, life did not return to normal. For a single mom of four, small children, living on public assistance, I do not think that normal was possible. Within two days, Megan experienced another crying episode, followed by an intense period to deep sleep. I called Dr. Schwartz, and he told me to bring Megan into his office immediately. After spending four days in the hospital and having Megan endure a myriad of tests, I was frustrated that we still didn't know what was happening to Megan when her little heart raced. That night in Dr. Schwartz's office, he figured it out.

While all six of us were in the office, Megan began to have another episode. Dr. Schwartz instinctively called a nurse to bring him a dish of ice, which he used to cool Megan's body. He said that her heart was racing, and he hoped that the coolness of the ice would stop the episode. He was exactly right. Dr. Schwartz diagnosed Megan with supraventricular tachycardia, a type of heart condition that was easily managed with digitalis, a drug generally prescribed for elderly heart patients. Some type of prenatal stress had likely been the cause of Megan's SVT, but with medication, regular monitoring, and proper follow-up with a children's cardiologist, Dr. Schwartz assured me that Megan would be just fine.

After four years of taking digitalis and having regular visits with a cardiologist, Megan no longer needed the medication. The doctors had predicted that her heart would grow stronger as she grew older and would no longer need medication, and they had been right on target. Megan has no long-term effects from her hospitalization. Thankfully, with good medical care and the diligence of my maternal instincts, Megan's medical problem was resolved. The medicaid coverage, which had been inadequate to supply proper prenatal care, which in turn likely contributed to the cause of Megan's heart problems, was at least sufficient to cover the care Megan needed to diagnose and cure her problem. I was very thankful for that.

Twelve

Real Life Law *v. L.A. Law*

It is a difficult lesson to learn. The reality of being involved in a court proceeding is very different than what might be seen on a television show or in a major motion picture. Sadly, many deserted, abandoned, and abused mothers and families take cases to court, relying on the idea that they will be granted justice, without understanding that real life law is not what is seen on T.V.

Societal trends and economic influences have altered the legal process over time. The law, as it is, does not financially punish people for bad behavior in a domestic situation. In the past, a spouse who committed adultery or deserted his family could be slapped with a very high financial price to pay for his conduct, in the form of a divorce decree granting most marital property to his deserted wife and children. Today, however, the distribution of marital property is more of a numbers game than an attempt to punish the spouse who caused the breakdown of a marriage and the destruction of the home of children.

Historically, domestic relations law was formulated to have a deterrent effect on parties. It was designed to keep families together by looming around, intangibly, silently reminding people that to engage in an extramarital affair, or to walk out on a family, would lead to a legal price too high to make any such behavior worthwhile. In today's celebrity-centered culture, divorce is a daily event. People enter into marriages with the expectation they will eventually divorce. Families are treated as temporary. Children are considered possessions rather than treasures. It is a sad state of affairs, and our country will pay the price.

Daily, I receive telephone calls from people who have been lied to, cheated, swindled, deserted, neglected, abandoned, thrown out of their homes, mistreated, conned, abused, and generally, made the victim of someone else's bad behavior. Unfortunately, television and the media have fostered an unrealistic expectation in all of us—the expectation that the law will protect us. The law will "fix it." The law will "make it right."

The law, however, is a system of rules, procedures, and requirements. It is designed to be objective and does not succumb to soap-opera-like stories. The law operates on facts and evidence. Compelling circumstances, no matter how sad and unfortunate, may not be legally persuasive.

I have engaged in court hearings where, clearly, one party was lying. I have engaged in a court hearing where one party admitted to not paying more than one hundred thousand dollars in child support to his children, yet, was able to have his child support obligation reduced. I have been in court hearings where blatantly abusive men were not found responsible for the abuse they caused, because their wives were too afraid to call the police immediately after a violent incident. I have been in a court hearing where visitation with his three-year-old daughter was granted to a formerly incarcerated, child sex-offender, because her mother had chosen to get involved with and have a child with, another incarcerated man.

The legal system is not perfect. The system does not always produce results that are just and grounded in truth. As human beings, we are fallible. No matter what safeguards are put into place to protect the integrity and validity of the legal process and our court system, there will always be someone who can get by the system, manipulate the system, abuse the system, overcome the system, or exploit the system. For the rest of us, we can learn the law, study the policies and procedures attached to it, collect our evidence, prepare our cases, and do our best to achieve a just result.

Real life law is not what is seen on T.V. Real life law is most often not as dramatic. Real life law is often not as swift. Real life law is frequently not fair. And, real life law might not end in justice. But, as citizens of the United States, we are each entitled to access the benefits and protections of our law. It is up to each of us to be diligent, to understand the law, and to use it wisely, prudently, and truthfully.

Thirteen

Why Don't You Go to Law School?

Two and one-half years passed. After some fifty appearances at the courthouse for hearings, or appointments, or attempts to work my support case, we were finally able to get off of welfare. Eric moved from his parents' home in Winchester, Virginia, to a tiny apartment in Berkley Springs, West Virginia. He obtained a job at the local Food Lion, making $7 per hour. It was not a lot, but Child Support Enforcement was at last able to set up a wage-withholding order. With the order in place, we received our first true support payment. Although there was a two-to three-week lag time between Eric's pay date and my receipt of the support check, it was wonderful to receive a check that was not, for the first time in almost three years, a welfare check. It was liberating and felt as though a heavy weight had been lifted off my shoulders. Finally, the state was not taking care of my kids, and I had my rights back. I intended to use those rights, act on those rights, and help others like me to do the same.

During one of our many child support hearings, I asked the court to find Eric criminally liable for refusing to provide the support to us that had been ordered by the court. Waiting for the Division of Child Support Enforcement to act was doing nothing more than keeping me on welfare. Accessing civil remedies for nonsupport required months of waiting for an initial status hearing. During a status hearing, a trial date, often several additional months away, would be set. All in all, a full year could pass before we would have a trial regarding Eric's refusal to pay the support. Also, Eric moved frequently. Since he did not maintain a stable residence, getting him properly served was a perpetual problem. Unless a party is formally served with a summons to appear in court for such a hearing, the hearing will not go forward. Without service, under the law, there would be no hearing.

We had many continuances in the support case due to the fact that Eric was difficult to serve. We also had continuances when I brought my children to court with me because I had no one to look after them on a particular day. Without my support money, I could not afford to hire a baby-sitter. I did informal baby-sitting at my church, Truro Church, in Fairfax, Virginia, to earn some money to pay for diapers, but without steady, substantial income, I couldn't waste one penny. On several occasions, when I appeared before the Honorable Arnold P. Kassabian in Fairfax County, he wouldn't hear me because I had the children along. He would put the case back on the docket for a future date, and I would have to wait, again, to be heard. I didn't argue with Judge Kassabian, but during the course of my many appearances before him, I openly questioned the law. I questioned the way the court managed child support cases, and was bold enough to remind him that the Virginia Code provided that nonsupport was a criminal offense in the Commonwealth. I even pleaded with him to help us.

At the last court appearance we had before the welfare checks stopped, Judge Kassabian encouraged me to pursue a career in law. Initially, he ruled against me in my effort to hold Eric criminally liable for nonsupport. Eric had testified that one afternoon he stopped by my home and ordered a pizza, and that he had shared that pizza with the children. The judge found that technically, even though Eric didn't pay the court-ordered support, he had provided something for the children—a few slices of pizza. Judge Kassabian went on to explain to me the difference between the standards of proof required for criminal cases and those required for civil cases. In a criminal case, the burden of proof is high—"Beyond a reasonable doubt." In a civil case, the burden of proof is easier—"By a preponderance of the evidence . . . that is, more likely to have occurred than not." It was my first formal lesson in the law. I took it to heart, understanding why the courts prefer civil proceedings to criminal proceedings in child support cases. With a lower burden of proof, the chances for conviction are higher. The process takes longer, but the final outcome is likely to be better for the children involved than the outcome in a criminal case would be. After all, an incarcerated parent is not going to be earning a lot of support money. It was after the judge had fully explained the reasoning behind his negative ruling, that he spoke directly to me and suggested that I consider going to law school. He said that I obviously had a good, working knowledge of the law and mentioned the John Marshall School of Law in Chicago, Illinois, indicating that he was confident that I could make it there.

I had been in front of Judge Kassabian repeatedly in my attempt to get off of welfare and force Eric to pay his lawfully owed support. In Fairfax County Juvenile and Domestic Relations Court, a case generally remains with the same judge. I tried criminal contempt, civil contempt, filing petitions for modification, and any other creative method of accessing the law that I could come up with. I visited the Fairfax County Law Library, located on the third floor of the county's primary courthouse. I pulled Virginia Code books, read through the family law sections, and tried to learn as much as I possibly could. Initially, I was learning out of necessity. Later, however, the necessity morphed into a passion to learn the law for the purpose of making it more accessible, more available, more practical, and more effective, especially for families like mine. In the aisles of that library, I found a calling. After years of not knowing what I wanted to do with my life, after dropping out of college and leaving the country to live with a virtual stranger, after marrying someone I hardly knew and becoming involved in a family situation full of heartache and self-focused adults, after having four children without a responsible father, after living hopeless and without resources on public assistance, I finally found a calling—a purpose for the madness that my life had become. I had to do whatever it took to act on that calling. It was the beginning of a long, and seemingly never-ending journey. My journey toward a career as a full-fledged attorney began in September 1991. It ended on October 6, 2001, with the news that I had passed the Virginia Bar exam. It had been a ten-year journey. But, it was worth every minute.

Although I completed an undergraduate degree, it took me seven years and five schools to do it. Between my anorexia, my succession of unrelated schools and majors, my dropping out, my getting married, my having four children, my husband's desertion, and our existence on welfare, my undergraduate record was weak to average, at best. Admission to a decent law school required solid academic credentials, superior law school admissions exam scores, excellent references, few outside obligations, money, and a good bit of luck. When I began my inquiries into actually attending law school, I had none of those things. I probably couldn't have gotten into a bad law school, never mind a good one. That was a fact. I accepted that fact, and, again, had to be creative.

I sat for the law school admissions exam twice. The first time, I prepared on my own. I gathered my sister's old study guide's from our parents' home, read the material whenever the kids were sleeping, and began to study at night after they went to bed. I pored through the outlines, made notes, and reviewed and rewrote the material, hoping to commit it to memory. I worked and studied hard to do well on the exam. Historically, I was not a good test taker. During my years of primary and secondary education I did well, but, I only did well because I worked so hard. I was not naturally smart. My sister was the naturally brilliant one. She always did well, and doing well was part of her nature. With me, doing well had to be almost forced. Anyway, my first set of scores were low-average to average—not dreadful, but also not worthy of admission to any law school that I knew of.

I had to take the exam again. This time, I enrolled in an exam preparation course at the University of Maryland's University College. The kids stayed with my parents all day, for two days, so that I could attend. At $165, the class was expensive, but after saving baby-sitting money for several months, I had enough to pay for it. It was tough to save the money; we could have used it for other things, but I looked at it as an investment in our future. The course was helpful—my score increased dramatically. It may not have been worthy of Harvard or Yale, but it was good enough to get me into some law school.

After my first try at the law school admissions exam, I applied to more than twenty law schools, and received more than twenty rejections. While at the exam preparation course, I learned about a legal fellowship program entitled "The Council on Legal Education Opportunity." If I could raise my score, I thought I might have a shot at the fellowship program. In addition, I applied to Georgetown University's legal assistant program. If I couldn't get into "real" law school, I figured I would start with the next best thing—paralegal school. I was accepted to the paralegal program and began the complicated process of seeking federal financial aid.

The classes were held downtown, in Washington, D.C. The program was eighteen months long. My tuition and books would be covered by financial aid, but baby-sitting was another problem. With classes four evenings a week, I had to find someone to take care of the children while I was at school. Class began at 6:00 P.M. To get to Georgetown by that time, I had to leave Centreville by five o'clock. Class ended at 9:40, which would mean I wouldn't be home until after 10:30. The schedule would be tough, but I had to figure out a plan. I had to do something to make it work.

I taught aerobics at a local church, and while I was there one morning, I read a note card posted on the church bulletin board, which indicated that a single mom of a three-month-old baby was looking for a "swapping" situation for day care services. Her name was Karen, and her baby's name was Jessica. I called Karen's telephone number that same evening, and we talked about her job and the day care needs she had. She had a job working for a local company as a receptionist, and her hours were 8:00 A.M. through 4:00 P.M. Her office was only about twenty minutes away from my home. If I cared for Jessica during the day, Karen could care for my kids at night, while I went to class.

Baby Jessica arrived at 7:30 each morning. I took all the children to Truro Church two mornings a week so I could baby-sit in the nursery during a ladies' Bible study. Two additional mornings a week, I packed up all five kids and went to another church to teach my aerobics class. One morning a week, we stayed at the house, took walks, and went to the grocery store when necessary. It wasn't easy taking care of five children under the age of four by myself.

Georgetown's paralegal program was intense. It involved nightly, detailed reading of hundreds of pages, writing long legal papers and memorandums, preparing legal research and reported cases for oral presentations, and spending significant time in law libraries reading case books and legal opinions. On Friday, Saturday, and Sunday evenings, I packed up the kids, filled my book bag with crackers, juice, a copy card, and a diaper bag, and drove to the George Mason University School of Law's Law Library in Arlington, Virginia. The kids brought their blankets. I would lead them to the stack where I needed to do research, and would have them sit down on the carpet between the stacks. I passed out the crackers and juice, pulled the volumes I needed from the shelves, and we all sat on the floor while I did my reading. The library was open until midnight on the weekends. We stayed out late, but, I had to get the reading done. Thankfully, the kids were always quiet. We were never asked to leave.

During the paralegal program, I became accustomed to studying late at night. After 10:30 or 11:00 P.M. I was pretty safe to assume that the kids would be asleep for a while. I needed complete quiet to study and write. Late at night, I always could find the quiet I needed to work. Sometimes, late at night, it was too quiet and my mind would drift off to Eric. I would wonder where he was and what he was doing. When it was dark and late and lonely, I often felt sorry for myself. In the loneliness of nighttime, it was easy to lose sight of my motivation and my goal, and I often longed for the normalcy of a family that had two parents and of a husband who actually cared for and took care of his family. The nights of longing were nothing more than wasted time. Eric would not magically change into the husband and father I wished for. With the help of several Pepsis and an occasional No Doz, I would bring myself back to reality, my work, and the task before me. If the Pepsi or No Doz didn't get me back into focus, it never failed that one of the kids would wake up just long enough for a diaper change or a drink—just long enough to remind me who and what I was working for and toward. My kids were such powerful motivation. My loneliness and my desire to have a normal, adult relationship didn't matter. I had brought my children into the situation, I had to do what was necessary to get them out of it.

I loved the course work. All of my professors were practicing attorneys, and I loved asking them questions. I soaked up the material presented in the classes and probably irritated my classmates with my nightly multitude of questions. I didn't care what my classmates thought, I had no choice but to make the most of every minute of every class. I could not afford to sleep during class. I had to learn the material right then and there. At home, there was no time to relearn what should have been learned in class. I had to discipline myself to focus on my work. No daydreaming. No mindless wandering. Every moment of class moved me, and more importantly the kids, a moment closer to a better life.

The spring came quickly. In May 1992, I was informed that I had been accepted into the 1992 Council on Legal Education Opportunity Fellowship Program to be held at Georgetown University Law Center in Washington, D.C. The purpose of the fellowship program was to provide an avenue for students who could represent underrepresented populations in the legal field, to be accepted into law school, in spite of less than stellar academic credentials. A CLEO fellow had to demonstrate the ability to do the legal work and have the motivation and drive to practice on behalf of persons traditionally underrepresented in the courts and legal process at large. After my experiences on welfare, I thought I would be ideal as a CLEO fellow. If I only had the opportunity to be a genuine law student, I could really make a difference. Things were looking up.

The kids and I were chosen by the local ABC Television News, News 7 of Washington, D.C., to be part of an election survey bit. The producers asked seven different families to share their opinions and concerns regarding the 1992 presidential elections during recurring television news segments. To get myself properly prepared for the segments, I wrote to presidential candidates George Bush and Bill Clinton. One afternoon during the spring of 1992, I discovered an official White House envelop in my mailbox. In the envelope was a letter from then President George Bush. The letter was written on thick, parchment-type, cream-colored stationery. Two and one-half pages were typed, one was handwritten. On the handwritten page, President Bush thanked me for writing and for working to help others. I had written to him about child support enforcement and welfare reform. In his response, he addressed increased efforts to enforce child support orders, particularly orders over state lines. The president also mentioned my four children. To receive that letter from the actual, sitting president of the United States, was one of the most important events of my lifetime. That afternoon, I took the kids to K-Mart and bought a simple, inexpensive frame for the letter. It has been prominently displayed in every house I have lived in since that memorable day.

The kids and I received a Section VIII federal housing voucher and were able to move into a single family home in Chantilly, Virginia. After I began the paralegal program at Georgetown and began caring for baby Jessica every day in exchange for evening child care, I didn't have enough income to pay the rent for our town house. Linda Crouch, my social worker at the Department of Family Services, worked tirelessly to help my family become involved with a transitional housing organization called Homestretch. Homestretch took over our lease, so technically, we became homeless, which enabled us to move up in priority on the waiting list for a Section VIII housing voucher.

A Section VIII housing voucher offered us the opportunity to rent a home and pay a straight percentage of our monthly income for rent. When Homestretch allowed us to become a part of its program, a doorway was opened for me to follow my newly developed passion for the law and advocacy to fruition. With a Section VIII voucher, our housing situation was secure. Even if our child support stopped completely, the rent would be altered to be a percentage of whatever income we actually received. One-third of zero income was zero. At last, my daily worries about housing for my family could be put away. We had a home and would not lose it.

Moving to our house in Chantilly took about two weeks. Eric helped me move our couches, beds, and large items. I rented a truck, and we worked all day. Eric seemed to want to be helpful. He liked the house, and I think, he actually felt a bit left out by not living there with us. The kids carried some of their toys and clothes. We had only about three miles to move, but the "stuff" in our house seemed to be never ending. Each time I thought I had packed everything from a room or a cabinet, I would find some other items lurking in the back of a closet or drawer. For almost two weeks, every day, I traveled back and forth between the two houses trying to transfer everything from one to the other. During the daytime, I set the kids in their car seats on the front sidewalk, while I packed the car with assorted things. Then, we drove to the new house and followed the same procedure while I unpacked the car. My mailman noticed how long it was taking me to accomplish the move. It was a few days before Christmas, and I had missed a week of classes, at a time when final exams were approaching fast. One Saturday morning, I heard a knock at the door. It was our wonderful mailman, who had driven a large, white mail truck over and offered to help me clear out the rest of the house. After working with me all morning and most of the afternoon, he gave me a Christmas card with a gift certificate to Giant Food Store enclosed. I was overwhelmed by his generosity.

Blessed by my sister, my parents, my friends, and the kindness of people like our mailman, we always had what we needed. Whether it was a real Christmas tree brought to our house by volunteers at Our Daily Bread, or a mysterious drop-off of groceries and goodies at our front door, or a magically appearing secret Santa from our church, we continued to be touched by the assistance of others. Having to accept help to meet basic needs was humbling and, sometimes, humiliating. But, the kids needed things I couldn't provide. I couldn't allow my ego or my poor choices or my inadequacies to interfere with the needs of the children. They had to come first.

Fourteen

The Summer of 1992

The summer of 1992 forever altered our lives. After I received an acceptance letter from the Council on Legal Education Opportunity program at Georgetown Law Center, I had to quickly figure out a way to attend six weeks of classes, all day at the law center, while continuing my evening paralegal classes at Georgetown University. The fellowship program met from ten to four every day, for six weeks. My paralegal classes were four nights a week from 6:00 until 9:40. I had to find care for the kids almost all day and all evening, four days a week for six weeks that summer. My mom agreed to take Megan and Tricia. My friend from Truro Church, Chris, offered to watch April and Phillip.

For six weeks, I got the children up at seven, drove April and Phillip over to Chris's house, drove Tricia and Megan to my mom's house, drove downtown for the fellowship program, returned to pick up the kids, brought everyone home to get settled in for the evening, put dinner out for the kids and the baby-sitter, headed back downtown for my night classes, returned home around 10:30 P.M. put the kids in the car to take the baby-sitter home, returned home to put the kids in their beds, and then, pulled out my reading and legal writing for both the fellowship program and my paralegal course work. Those six weeks during the summer of 1992 were both the longest, and the shortest, weeks of my life.

The alleged payoff for that summer of 1992, was the promise of a seat in the first year class of a local law school plus access to substantial financial aid. The rough schedule of that summer was a small burden to bear in light of the opportunity it afforded me, and through me, the kids. My undergraduate record and mediocre exam scores wouldn't get me into a D.C. area law school. The fellowship program was the best shot I had at achieving my goal. I successfully completed the six week program, received my certificate of completion, and waited to hear where I would be placed. Several weeks passed, with no news coming from the CLEO office. I began to call, daily, to find out what was happening with my promised placement. It was the middle of August, and all of the D.C. law schools were beginning first year orientation programs. All the other CLEO fellows had their seats and were already in class.

After another week of consistent calling to the CLEO office, I was told that my paperwork and application materials had been misplaced. Although I had successfully completed the fellowship program, it was too late to receive a fall placement. I was effectively shut out from law school after a summer of daily determination and sacrifice—not just on my part but on my children's as well. The acting dean for admissions at Georgetown Law Center and the director of the fellowship program assured me that I could use my CLEO fellowship materials to reapply to law school the next year. But, that was not good enough. That was not what I had been promised. I filed a lawsuit against Georgetown Law Center and the fellowship program in an attempt to receive a seat that fall at Georgetown.

Although I got my day in court, the judge who heard my case found that since classes were already under way, and had been for a number of weeks, I would have to reapply and wait until the following year, anyway. All of the work and the driving and the sleepless nights—all for nothing.

I fell into a deep depression after my lawsuit was dismissed. Although I still had my paralegal program to complete, I had been so focused, so certain that I was destined to be a lawyer. When my CLEO fellowship failed to get me a seat in law school, all of my hopes for the future, my mental justifications for all of the hard times the children and I had, crumbled into pieces. While I was at one of my lowest points since having anorexia, Eric called.

We had not seen him since shortly after our last move. He was still living in West Virginia, working at Food Lion, and didn't have a car. I don't know why, but I broke down on the phone and told him how wrong everything had gone. He invited us to come to Berkeley Springs for a visit. The kids had gone a long time without seeing Eric, and he was, after all, their dad. I decided that if my opportunity to be a lawyer and take care of my kids properly was nothing more than a far away, unattainable dream, I could at least try to respond to Eric's request. Maybe he had changed? Ever since his hospitalization for depression in 1988, I had constantly prayed that he would one day change. I never wanted to be divorced. I had meant my vows when I said them. I was not a quitter.

I packed the car, as I always did, with the car seats, crackers, juice, the diaper bag, and a few pieces of extra clothing, and we headed off to Berkeley Springs, not knowing what to expect. To my surprise, Berkeley Springs was quaint and lovely. Eric's apartment was located on a major truck route, and was located above a little, old-fashioned diner. Down the street was Berkeley Springs, a real freshwater spring. We met Eric in the diner and walked up the street to the spring. The water was ice-cold, crystal clear, and full of shiny, colored guppies. The kids had fun touching the spring water, drinking out of a faucet that was attached to a large gray rock, and watching the guppies swim around the pool of water that gathered from the spring's outpouring of water.

After walking outside for a couple of hours, the kids were tired and ready to eat. We stopped at a small pizza parlor and ordered take-out for dinner. The food in Berkeley Springs was inexpensive. While we were there, we went shopping at Food Lion. I still qualified for food stamps and could purchase more food in Berkeley Springs with my allotment than I could purchase back home in Chantilly. Eric's cabinets were empty. I felt sorry for him and bought him some food, along with cleaning supplies for his apartment. The apartment was small, and it's windows had no screens. The exhaust from the trucks passing by traveled up through the air and wafted into the front windows. After we ate the pizza, I cleaned the bathroom with bleach and gave the kids a bath. The kids were obviously tired. Eric set out a big comforter in his bedroom for the kids to lay down on. They were all asleep in no time.

It was the last night of the Republican national convention. Ronald Reagan was the keynote speaker. I loved to listen to Ronald Reagan. When I was a senior in high school, I saw him in person when he came to my church for the funeral of the son of his attorney general, Ed Meese. Eric sat down next to me on the couch. The apartment reminded me of our apartment in Germany. We watched the convention, talked some political small talk, and, found ourselves like we used to be when we were first married—during the first few weeks—when things were actually good. It was just one night. It wasn't real. But, seventeen weeks later, still as much a single mother as ever, I discovered that I was pregnant, again. We had been separated more than two and a half years, I was on welfare, and, I was pregnant again. I had become one of "those welfare mothers" I heard about on television. I was petrified and more humiliated than I ever imagined I could be.

Karen moved away from the area, and my evening baby-sitting arrangement fell apart. Thankfully, lots of teenagers who were willing to baby-sit lived in my neighborhood. My task was to find one that could handle four little kids under the age of four. We made about six or seven different tries before we found Lauren. Lauren was a high school junior who reminded me of me when I was her age. She was ultimately responsible, worked for the school newspaper, was great with the kids, and always left the house in better condition than it was when she came over. I was able to finish my paralegal program, and I reapplied to every law school I had ever applied to before. I denied that I was pregnant until I saw the new baby on a sonogram. That pregnancy was different from the others. I taught aerobics and didn't have any symptoms of being pregnant for several months after that night in Berkeley Springs. Maybe I knew subconsciously, but I didn't want to believe it on a conscious level.

I confided in my friend Chris. She was such a source of encouragement and rational thinking for me. After her constant help and support during the fellowship program, I knew I had a true friend in Chris, so I went to her for help after the ultrasound. She talked to me calmly. I was so afraid of what my parents and family would say. They had already seen me through so much. I had disappointed them, but they stood by me, anyway. What would they say or do now? Five children. No dad to speak of. No viable source of income. Once again, my situation was worse than I could have imagined it could ever be.

No acceptances to law school arrived in the mail. As time passed, my pregnancy became obvious. I was embarrassed and tried to hide my widening stomach and backside. But my mother figured it out, and my parents were extremely upset. We didn't speak for several months. I kept to myself for most of my pregnancy. Chris agreed to be in the delivery room with me. I literally tried to hide during the fall and winter of 1992–1993. Eric had disappeared again. I stayed in the house with the kids and tried to imagine our future. Would we be on welfare forever? How could I ever make things better with five children under the age of five and no help at home? My dream of law school was shattered; I must have had everything all wrong.

I spent months wallowing in embarrassment and fear. I became a recluse in my own house and dragged the kids down with me. Although I kept them in their preschool programs at Truro Church and continued baby-sitting as much as possible, emotionally, I was falling apart. When I went grocery shopping and felt that a cashier was looking at us dubiously or with some sort of disdain, I spontaneously spilled out my story. I told complete strangers that I was a single mom of five, that my husband deserted us, that I had no resources of my own, and that I had to use food stamps to feed my kids. Looking back, I am certain that the cashiers had no desire to hear my tale of woe. I have no idea why I would spout out the sordid details of my life, but I did. I guess it was my way of coping.

In February 1993, Mrs. Angela Mynns, the wife of the rector at our church, did something for me that put my focus and my life back on track. I confided in Angela about my unexpected pregnancy. She hugged me and told me it would be OK and that she was happy for me, and she encouraged me to be happy, too. She reminded me of the blessings and opportunities offered by a new life. One afternoon following a morning of baby-sitting at the church nursery, Angela surprised me with a baby shower. I never expected anyone to have a baby shower for me. I had been so bogged down in my embarrassment, that I had completely neglected the joy and promise of the new life I carried within me. I will never forget that baby shower. Angela specifically invited my mom and took care to smooth things out for us as best she could. I received wonderful gifts. We ate delicious food. It was a very special day. It was a day that brought me back to reality and prompted me to get back on track toward building a better life for my family.

Later that February, I went into premature labor. I called Chris, and she immediately drove to my house, called my doctor, helped get the children in the car, and took me to the hospital. My ultrasound showed that I was having a boy. The ultrasound also showed that February was too soon for the baby to be born. He needed more time. My doctor was great. She worked in the Fairfax Family Practice. She was kind and patient, and understanding. She admitted me into the hospital, put me on IVs, and told me to rest and try to take better care of myself, if not for me, then for the baby. And, for the other kids.

My mom kept the children for the four days I was in the hospital. I knew that it was not easy for her to take care of all four at once. They were a handful. Just the feeding and diaper changing of all four was time consuming. While I was in the hospital, it snowed and the World Trade Center in New York City was bombed. It was a time full of turmoil, but my several days in the hospital gave me a good opportunity to do some objective thinking. I could wallow in self-pity and embarrassment, or, I could direct my energy toward a better purpose. If I wanted to ruin my own life, that was one thing, but, to ruin the lives of my children was unacceptable. I had no choice but to get myself together, improve my education, figure out a way to earn a decent income, and move on with life.

Fifteen

Lawn Mowing and Labor

My neighbor Brooks and I had an ongoing, silent competition. Each week, we tried to beat each other to the punch when it came to having our lawns mowed and trimmed. I loved to mow the lawn; it provided me with an instant sense of accomplishment. As I looked over my green yard, with its neatly sheared rows and carefully trimmed edges, I felt an immediate satisfaction of a job well done. It was a type of escape. The noise of the motor carried me away to another world—to a place where I could think clearly and thoughtfully. Nothing could get in the way of my lawn mowing schedule. I was compulsive about it. In my life of uncertainty and continued turmoil, mowing my yard every week gave me a sense of routine, a type of control. It was almost therapeutic.

I put my hopes for law school away and focused on surviving. Our home was secure as long as my landlord didn't sell the house. April and Tricia were at preschool at Truro Church via scholarships. My parents paid for Phillip to go to kindergarten, and Megan was home with me. We continued to receive our child support, as long as Eric stayed with Food Lion. The children and I remained on Medicaid, and, because of our low income, we continued to qualify for food stamps. Our basic needs were always met. I spent the early months of 1993 just waiting for the arrival of baby number five, while keeping my other children clothed, fed, and occupied.

Living in a single-family home was great. Our house sat on a lot at the left-rear of a cul-de-sac. The yard was fairly large and gave the kids plenty of room to play ball and play on a swing-set. With a yard of our own, we planted flowers, ran through sprinklers, pulled weeds, and mowed at least weekly. At first I was afraid to have a gas-powered mower with several small children around. I had heard too many stories about kids getting hurt by their fast-moving, razor-sharp blades. To avoid the possibility of an accident, I bought a manual lawn mower. When the mower was new and the blades could actually cut the grass, I was able to get the yard mowed in about three hours, and because it was manual, the mower made no noise, so I could cut the grass while the kids slept inside the house.

After a few weeks of use, the mower became dull and would not cut the grass at all. Walking up and down the yard with the dull mower, I accomplished nothing more than pushing the blades of grass over, only to have them pop right back to an upright position. I had to give in and buy a power lawn mower. I found one at Montgomery Wards. My sister, Patti, had given me a Montgomery Wards charge card to use for clothing and household items. Megan and I went to buy the mower one morning when the other kids were at school. The mower was a great price—only $109. But, there was a caveat to that great price; the unit came unassembled—in about fifty pieces, with seventy-five screws. I pushed the box into the back of the car, buckled Megan into her car seat, and drove home to begin my adventure in lawn mower assembly.

My attempts to be a handyman around the house were usually unsuccessful. I was definitely not mechanically inclined, and although I loved to watch Bob Villa and *This Old House,* I was no Tim the Tool Man Taylor. One February afternoon, I tried to light a fire in the old, cast-iron stove insert in the fireplace. To my horror, as I stacked a too-large log on top of kindling and newspaper, the log ignited prematurely. I yelled to the kids to open the back patio door, I grabbed the flaming log, ran across the room, out the door, and threw the log over the deck railing into the snow. The fire was out. But, I decided that fires in my house were not a good thing. I obviously could not get a fire going properly in my fireplace and could not risk the house catching on fire.

Another example of my lack of home-care prowess was when I attempted to paint the downstairs powder room in the house.

There had been a serious water leak in the plumbing system due to weak pvc piping. As a result, several water springs popped up in the front yard and the ceiling of the downstairs powder room collapsed. Fortunately, none of the kids were in the powder room when the ceiling fell down. My landlord was not extraordinarily helpful when it came to household repairs. He would not hire outside help and always either tried to do repairs himself, or had one of his grown sons do them. After the ceiling came down, my landlord's son pulled out the drywall and rebuilt the bathroom walls from scratch. New walls were put up, but the work had been crudely done and the walls were left unpainted.

I didn't like the unpainted walls. In my effort to improve the aesthetics of that room, I took the kids with me to Hechinger's, our local hardware store, to pick out and buy paint that would brighten up the bathroom and the adjacent area. Needing to spend as little as possible, I went to the shelves containing paint that had been left over from custom-mixed paint orders. I found a shade of mauve that, from the sample on the lid of the can, appeared to be perfect, soft, but slightly pink. I bought the paint and a couple of large, soft paintbrushes and took my items home. I worked for three days painting the bathroom. I painted carefully and covered every piece of exposed wall. When the work was complete, the bathroom looked like a fluorescent, hot-pink box. The color was much too loud for that small room and, took four coats of new, off-white paint to hide it.

After trying for three mornings, I was finally able to put my new lawn mower together. With the last wheel in place, I added a bit too much oil and then gassed the mower up and pulled the starter cord. It took about twelve tries before the motor fired up, and I was growing more frustrated with each pull. But, when the motor, at last, kicked on and stayed on, I steered it out to the yard and began to cut the grass in even, parallel rows. Several hours passed, and I had to leave my mowing project to pick the kids up from school. When we returned, I went back to my mowing, while the kids played in the yard. Although lawn mowing was time consuming and was especially difficult after a rain, I enjoyed the simplicity of mowing the yard, the opportunity to escape into the noise of the engine, and the ability to accomplish a task and be with the children at the same time.

The afternoon I went into labor with my son Thomas, I was mowing the yard. I was more than nine months pregnant and had been ordered to bed rest weeks earlier. Bed rest was not possible with four small children to care for alone. I was careful, but work had to be done, and as long as the needs of the kids never rested, neither did I. Phillip, April, Tricia, and Megan were playing in the yard while I mowed that April afternoon. I began to have steady, consistent contractions at about four o'clock that afternoon. After having had four previous inductions, I was certain that this labor would also be slow to move ahead. I didn't worry about the pains and continued to mow. Finally, at about 6:30, the contractions became too uncomfortable for me to continue mowing. I went inside the house, quickly called our family practice, and asked to speak with my doctor. She calmly, but firmly, advised me to get to the hospital as soon as possible.

I called my mom and my friend Chris. I put the lawn mower away, cleaned up the yard, and brought the children inside. The kids were dirty after playing outside so I gave them each a bath and packed several small bags with their clothes, bottles, a few toys, and diapers. Then, I took a shower, packed a bag for myself, put everyone and everything in the car, and drove to my mom's home in Vienna, Virginia. My mom helped me get the kids and their things out of the car, and she took them inside the house, and I drove on to the hospital. I arrived at the Fairfax Hospital around ten o'clock. My doctor had been waiting for several hours and was worried because it had taken me so long to get to the hospital.

The doctor had a room ready for me in labor and delivery. While spending so much time arranging things so I could get to the hospital, I had failed to recognize the seriousness and life-changing nature of giving birth to my fifth child. I chose the name Thomas George. George was my maternal grandfather's name, and I always used a family name for my children. It was important to me that they have a name with a family connection. The name "Thomas George" was the name of a baby on my favorite show at the time, *Sisters*. The circumstances surrounding Thomas's birth were quite lonely and sad, but Thomas brought me joy and happiness and comfort and purpose at a particular time when I really needed all those things.

My doctor began to induce labor at midnight. I called the telephone number I had for Eric to let him know that I was about to have the baby. His landlord answered the phone, and with disgust in his voice, told me that he was "tired of taking calls like this so late at night," and hung up the phone. I heard nothing from Eric until Thomas was almost three months old. My friend Chris arrived thirty minutes later and stayed with me all night long until Thomas was born at 7:20 A.M. He was perfect—no problems, no worries. The delivery went well, and afterward, I felt reenergized and remotivated to get a new plan together so that I could provide a decent future for my family. My stay in the hospital was uneventful and a bit lonely. My mom and the kids came to visit the day after Thomas was born. My dad was out of town, so it was difficult for her to get around with all four children in tow. She did very well with the kids, but I couldn't ask her to bring them all out together by herself very often.

I walked Thomas around the maternity floor in his plastic bassinet, just as I had done with each of my previous children. I preferred to keep my babies with me at all times while we were in the hospital. I felt safer and more secure knowing the children were with me. Plus, those couple days in the hospital were the only ones I would ever have completely alone with each of my kids. I treasured that time. It was depressing to me, though, to watch other moms, new babies, families, and dads as they gathered as family units to celebrate the birth of their respective new family members. For most of our hours in the hospital, Thomas and I were alone. We had no dad there to celebrate with us. As I walked around the floor of the hospital unit, I watched joyful, proud fathers lovingly admire their new babies through the glass of the nursery windows. How I longed for Eric to be there to look at Thomas like that. While I slept at the hospital, with Thomas at my side, I dreamed of what it would be like to actually have a husband who cared, and doted, who was responsible and who was proud to be a father. When I woke up, I was quickly reminded of our reality. We were alone. We were without a husband and a father. Thomas would have me, and Phillip, and April, and Tricia, and Megan, and our extended family, but he wouldn't have a dad. And again it struck me that I had made the choices that had led us to that moment. It was my job to make things better for Thomas, and for all of us.

Two days after Thomas was born, it was time to go home. My dad was still out of town, and my mom was busy with Phillip, April, Tricia, and Megan. I packed up our things, gathered our hospital goodie bag of samples, diapers, and snacks, and got ready to go home. A nurse arrived at my room with a wheelchair and a cart for our bags and personal items, and Thomas and I rode down to the front of the hospital, pushed by the nurse. Arriving at the front lobby, I stood up and asked the nurse to hold Thomas while I went to the parking garage to get my car. It was time to begin my new life as a single parent of five. No one was available to give us a ride home that day, so I had no choice but to drive myself. The nurse that brought us downstairs told me that no new mother she knew of had ever driven herself and her baby home from the hospital. I guess I was their first. Because driving my car was against the medical advice of my doctor, I was required to sign a release form and statement that I was acting contrary to medical advice. I quickly signed the form and walked to the garage, where I found my car exactly as I had left it.

I rented a baby bucket car seat from the hospital, signed the billing paperwork for medicaid, put my flowers, bags, and Thomas in the car, and we drove to my parents' home in Vienna to pick up the other kids, to thank my mom for her help, and to return home to our new life as a family of six.

I kept Thomas's bassinet in the family room. Our kitchen overlooked the family room, and the two rooms together formed the central living area in that house. It was great to have a single family home, but, I had some serious concerns about safety and security. On several occasions, neighborhood kids had run up to my front door late at night and knocked. I know they really meant no harm, but their mischievous behavior gave me cause to feel unsafe sleeping upstairs in the master bedroom. For that reason, I slept on the couch in the family room. I guess it was a bit odd to sleep on the couch when I had a nice queen-size bed and my own room upstairs, but, every time I tried to stay upstairs for the night, I couldn't sleep. So, I spent my nights on the couch. The kids had a habit of sleeping on the family room floor in their sleeping bags. There was no need for them to sleep on the floor, but often, they watched television and fell asleep. Although it was probably laziness on my part, I usually allowed them to remain asleep in their sleeping bags for the night. With five small children, it was difficult to have a traditional bedtime routine. Gathering all five around in one place, to read one book, at one time, was pretty much an impossibility.

We fell into a routine of being a family of six without too much strife. I was fortunate because none of the kids experienced jealousy or resentment when a new member of the family joined us. During undergraduate child development classes, I had studied sibling rivalry. Growing up, I hadn't experienced sibling rivalry—my sister and I always seemed to get along well. Generally, we had different interests; we never had reason to compete with each other. As adults, our relationship has been even better. My brother and I, on the other hand, never seemed to get along. It was not a rivalry or a competition, he just never liked me, and, that continues to this day.

To have five children is an amazing thing. When I see other people with four, I think to myself, "That is a lot of kids." When I observe a group of six people, it doesn't seem possible that my kids and I form a crowd the same size. But, I am blessed. My children get along with each other, have always been kind to each other, care about each other, and are generally pleasant to be around. Without my kids, I don't know where I'd be, who I'd be, or, if I'd be. They are everything to me.

Sixteen

Good-bye Grandpa

For several years, my sister and I traveled with the kids, during either the early summer or after Christmas, to visit our maternal grandparents in Rhode Island. I was the first grandchild in the family. My father's mother, to whom I was especially close, died when I was twelve. My mother's parents lived in a small New England town, a town filled with ice-cream shops and warmed by the aroma of clam cakes and the friendly smiles of its long-time residents.

During the Christmas season of 1993, Thomas's first Christmas, Patti and I drove to Rhode Island to visit Grandma and Grandpa. Our long car rides were great adventures. We traveled with four car seats and a booster seat, a playpen, assorted diaper bags, and, most important, a porta-potty. More than once, we had to pull over on a New York thruway near a newly stripped, abandoned automobile so that one or more of the kids could use the porta-potty. Looking back, although those trips were long and filled with too many rest stops, they were funny and forever memorable.

Our 1993 Christmas trip was a difficult trip for all of us, especially the kids. The Events of that Christmas led to my children's first experience with death. It was a moment I was not prepared for, and surprisingly, the kids handled it better than I did. When we arrived in Rhode Island on a damp, cold December night, my grandfather was already in the hospital. He had a round, youthful face and was always young at heart. He was ninety-two, and he was tired.

Although we only saw Grandpa once or twice a year, the children, especially April, were very attached to him. I named Thomas after him and was happy that he was able to meet and hold all of my kids before he died. It was Grandpa who had suggested the name "April" for my first daughter. April loves to hear the story of his suggestion, and I think his naming her was the foundation for the extra attachment April felt toward him.

We all went to the hospital to see him. The kids were all too young to go into the ward where he was. Patti and I took turns going into the hospital room and alternated watching the kids. Our family friend Clint was along on the trip and helped with the kids as well. It was tough to see Grandpa in the hospital. He was curled up on the bed and seemed so tired. He thought I was my mom at first, and when I told him who I was, he asked for her. When I explained to him that Patti and I were there with the kids, he asked to see them. The nurses would only allow Phillip to go back into the ward, so Phillip walked into the room and briefly visited with Grandpa and me. When we left Rhode Island that Christmas, in my heart I feared I would not see him again.

My fear became reality on a spring day in March 1994. Grandpa's health declined steadily after Christmas. The kids and I were at my parents' home when my mom received the final phone call. When I got the news that Grandpa was gone, my heart sank, my throat filled with a hard lump, and I knew I had to go to Rhode Island.

My mother always said that his only wish was to see me graduate from high school. Although he did see me graduate from high school, I knew that he worried about me and the kids. I had desperately wanted to get things together and make a secure life for my children while he was still alive. That did not happen.

My first thought was of how I could get to Rhode Island for the funeral. The kids and I were at my parents' house. My parents and I were in their kitchen when my sister called. When I told her that I wanted to take the kids to the funeral, she offered to come home, rent a car, and drive us there together. My dad said that it was impractical for me to go and suggested that Patti fly to Rhode Island from Los Angeles. He said since I had so many small children, and so few resources, I should stay home. I was terribly upset. I put the children in the car and drove home crying.

As I drove, my thoughts were scattered. I remembered a cold morning several years earlier when there had been a loud knock at my door at 5:30 in the morning. I always slept on the couch, because I was too nervous at night to sleep in an upstairs bedroom. If there happened to be a fire or an intruder, I wanted to be in the middle of the house so I could get everyone out quickly. When I heard the knock, I jumped up immediately. I looked out the side of the front window and saw Eric standing there with his head hanging down.

I opened the door to see him still looking down with water dripping from his face. He was crying. It was only the second time I had ever seen him cry. The first time was years earlier, immediately after Phillip was born. It was my sister's college graduation, and I was determined to go. Things were strained with Eric; we had just been through a traumatic time with Billy and Eric's parents. I wanted to get away from the entire mess for a while. I packed the car, packed up Phillip, and planned to go to the graduation by myself. Eric wanted to go with me. The first time I saw him cry was when I left that June for the graduation. He cried and asked me not to leave him, but I needed to get away, for just a couple of days.

That morning at 5:30, Eric was crying for a different reason. His grandmother had died. She was his mother's mother. Although he was pretty much removed from his family and did not have substantial ongoing relationships with any family member, he had been attached to his grandmother. I don't know why he came to see me that morning. I opened the door, he looked up, told me that his grandmother had died, and put his head on my shoulder. Although my common sense screamed inside my head that I should throw him out, that he didn't care about us, I let him stay for a few hours, and we talked about his grandmother. I could tell he was feeling a cold and empty kind of loneliness.

My thoughts then returned to the present. I was feeling a cold and empty kind of loneliness. I longed for someone to go to so that I could put my head on a shoulder and cry. But Eric was not there for me, and although I was surrounded by five small children, I felt amazingly alone. My grandfather was gone, and I feared that I would not be able to go to his funeral. I had to go and say good-bye.

I pulled into the garage and helped the kids out of the car. It was now late in the afternoon. They were hungry and tired. I put together something simple for dinner, got everyone fed, ran all the baths, and settled them down in front of *The Sound of Music,* their favorite video at the time. Then, I called my sister. I told her what my dad had said about the practicalities of my going to the funeral. As always, she told me not to worry about it and that "of course" I should go and that she would come home, rent a car, pick the kids and me up, and we would go together. Her help at the particular time was an enormous relief and a tremendous blessing. I did not want to miss that funeral.

Our trip to Rhode Island was relatively uneventful. Our purpose was somber, even the kids seemed to have a sense that the trip was not for fun. Phillip threw up in the car on our way up. Patti's coat took the brunt of it, but after a few years of being around us, she was used to such occurrences. After we arrived and settled into the hotel, we went to visit my grandmother. She was devastated. My grandfather had been the center of her life for more than fifty years. I always thought that a relationship like theirs was incredibly enviable and rare. To be with and committed to someone for so long was so ideal, and the idea so comforting. I knew that I would never have a relationship like that with Eric. I couldn't imagine the profound sadness my grandmother was experiencing. She was lost. She had never driven a car. She didn't have a checking account of her own. My grandfather had always been her rock and took care of everything. The kids and I visited with her and tried to comfort her. Then, we returned to the hotel. Funeral plans were not for kids. We would attend the viewing and the service, but we stayed at the hotel, and the kids swam in the pool while the rest of the family handled the details.

With little income and lots of responsibility, I felt bad that I couldn't contribute in a financial, tangible way to the expenses involved in my grandpa's funeral. My mom called me at the hotel and said that my grandmother wanted me to sing a song at the service. Although I had sung in choirs for years in school and had sung at a wedding or two in the past, I had not sung in front of a group of people for several years. I nervously agreed to sing. If I could not help with the expenses, I could at least contribute to the service in some way. I found the song, "Amazing Grace" and practiced in an upper room at the funeral home praying that I would sound OK.

The second day we were in Rhode Island, the children and I went to the open viewing. At the viewing, I saw my aunt and two uncles. Although as a child I had regularly seen my aunt and uncles during summer vacations, I had not seen them very often since graduating from high school. It was good to see extended family. I also saw one of my three cousins. He was a grown man, quite different from the teenage boy I remembered. Time had passed. We all were so much older, and Grandpa was gone. It was rough. I had only lost one immediate family member, my paternal grandmother, before the death of my grandfather. I was not good at handling difficult situations. My kids handled it better than I did.

My sister and I explained to them that Grandpa was gone, and that although we could see his body in the casket, he was already in heaven with God. The funeral service was held in the chapel of the funeral home. My dad wasn't sure the kids should attend, but with Patti and Clint there to help look after them, we decided that everyone should attend.

I remember it being a bright, cool morning as we drove to the funeral home. The kids were dressed nicely—Phillip in a button-down shirt and tie, April in patent leather shoes we had picked up at a children's consignment shop in Warwick. We rode in a mini-van with my brother. After arriving at the funeral home, I went into a room to practice my song. My grandmother seemed so despondent, I didn't know what to say to her.

The chapel was small, but quiet and tasteful. The room was quite full. My grandfather had been well known in Warwick, a charter member and founder of his church. He had been an avid bowler and had many friends. He had also been my grandmother's life. The pastor handed me a paper program and told me he would quietly acknowledge me when it was time to sing. I stood in the back of the chapel with the kids. I held Thomas; he was just under a year old. The service was brief, respectful, and a lovely tribute to my grandpa. Just as the pastor acknowledged me to begin my song, Thomas began to fuss. Patti and Clint watched over the children while I walked to a small podium to begin "Amazing Grace." After I made it half-way through the first phrase of the song, Thomas began to fuss louder. Then he crawled across the floor to where I was standing and sat quietly at my feet while I finished the song. The service ended.

We all returned to our rented cars and followed each other to Highland Memorial Park in Johnston, Rhode Island. There was to be no graveside service. Instead, we gathered in the chapel, the pastor offered a few words of scripture and comfort, and then everyone left. Everyone except the kids. April, Phillip, and Tricia walked over to the casket, put their hands on it, recited a brief prayer they had learned at Truro preschool, and said, "good-bye" to Grandpa. At ages five, six, and four, respectively, they made me very proud.

Seventeen

Capitol Hill

I had to be a part of the process. I studied the proposed bills, and I knew that most of the legislators on Capitol Hill, particularly the men, didn't have a clue. I was invited, under the Democratic leadership, to testify before Congress at the first set of welfare reform hearings held in July 1994. After my initial appearance (where I used outtakes of the film *Kramer vs. Kramer* to make my point), Congressman and Chairman of the House Ways and Means Committee Sam Givens, invited me to return to Capitol Hill to share my insights and experiences with members of his committee. That meeting never occurred. The Congress became Republican-led, and the welfare reform process began anew. It was OK, though. I was invited back under the Republican leadership, and this time, the *Washington Post* went with me.

While Thomas was an infant, I tried to find employment. I applied with day care centers, thinking that I could work at a center, bring my children with me, and also earn income that we desperately needed. I was surprised to learn that at every center I contacted, I would end up having to pay the center to work there. Although I could bring one child at no cost, my additional children could attend at a reduced rate only. With pay of $7 per hour, I would take home nothing.

We no longer qualified for food stamps because of the vehicle I drove. When my mom purchased a new car in 1994, my parents gave me her used minivan. It was wonderful to have a minivan. Our burgundy minivan had plenty of room for our five car seats and assorted child-related paraphernalia. The value of the car, though, was more than $2,500. A food stamp recipient, under federal law, could not own assets valued in excess of $2,500. To have such an asset was to be disqualified from the food stamp program. Initially, I was afraid to not have the safety net of our food stamp allotment. We needed the car, but the kids also needed to eat. Thankfully, with frequent baby-sitting at the church and careful food buying habits, we always had enough food in the house.

When things were extremely tight, I visited a local food pantry in Centreville, Virginia. The pantry was staffed and maintained by the Western Fairfax Christian Ministries. A small building was set up like a convenience store, and people like me, who could show a proper picture form of identification, were allowed to visit once every two weeks to "shop" for groceries. They had canned goods, dry goods, meat, fresh fruit, pastas, juices, and sometimes even diary items. The best thing about the food pantry was that the volunteers always treated pantry patrons with dignity and respect. The toughest part about asking for and accepting help was the reaction of the party being asked.

Many single moms I met through the church or community organizations or through the referral of a mutual friend were too embarrassed to seek out assistance with food, rent, or anything. Many single moms I met had suffered overwhelming humiliation and embarrassment after being deserted or abandoned by their husbands or boyfriends. Most could not bear any additional humiliation. Sadly, children and families often go without available resources because a despondent and exasperated single parent is too discouraged to seek those resources.

My efforts to obtain employment were unsuccessful. Child care for five children ages five and under was approximately $650 per week in Fairfax County, Virginia. The local Office for Children offered child care assistance, but the waiting list was two years long. Our needs could not wait for two years. I had to do something immediately to bring money into our home so that we could afford food, rent, and heat. After researching various options and checking into the availability of financial aid for graduate studies, I determined that the only way I could bring more money into our family to meet basic needs, was to go to graduate school.

As a graduate student with young children, I could qualify for student loans sufficient to cover tuition, books, transportation, child care, food, rent, utilities, and common everyday expenses. I knew that my student loan debt would eventually be enormous. But, I had no other option; the only way to survive was to seek out and obtain financial aid. Besides, I could obtain an advanced degree that—surely—would quality me for a good-paying job once the kids were all at school.

I applied to be a graduate student at National-Louis University, located in Northern Virginia. I was again faced with a large exam, but I did surprisingly well the first time out. It was the Miller Analogies Test, and I scored a 98 percent. I was pleased, was accepted into the program, and began work on my master's thesis. My work on the thesis project led me to become a proactive welfare reform and child support advocate. The thesis had to satisfy substantial writing and research requirements to meet the criteria necessary for the receipt of a master's degree in management. The program was such that I was in class all day, every Saturday, and worked on the thesis independently. Saturdays were difficult for the kids. I was able to find a terrific friend, Linda, in the neighborhood who worked as a mother's helper in addition to raising her four children. Linda worked as our child care provider for almost a full year, while I attended graduate school. When the needs and schedules of her family members changed, I found alternative child care for the kids and was able to complete the master's program in June of 1995.

While conducting research for my thesis, I began to write and submit editorial pieces to local newspapers. I gained a great deal of factual and statistical knowledge about welfare reform and child support enforcement. The reality of my experiences with welfare and child support did not contradict what the politicians and general public assumed was going on within our welfare system. With the knowledge I gained and the experience I lived, I knew I could make a difference. I knew I could get through to the legislators and policymakers who were in a position to revamp the system if I could figure out a way to be heard.

My writing became my avenue to advocacy. Whenever I thought of an idea or an analogy or a new way of educating the general public about the realities of welfare, I sat down and wrote. Whenever I saw a television show or news report about the topic, I sat down and wrote. I used my writing for the submission requirements related to my thesis, and then, I began to send copies of my pieces to local and national newspapers. The stereotypical representations of "welfare mothers" that filled reports on *20/20, 48 Hours, Dateline NBC, Nightline, 60 Minutes,* and all of the morning and evening daily news shows filled me with anger and resolve. Anger at the simplistic exacerbation of stereotypes. Resolve to do something to get the truth out to the public.

The average "welfare mother" in the United States during the year 1994–95 was a twenty-six-year-old, divorced, mother of two, not a teenage mother. Not a mother of ten children with eleven possible fathers. Not a never-married mother. But, a young, formerly married mother of two children who found herself alone to care for and raise the children after her husband had abandoned them. I was that mother, with three additional children. I was determined to "get the truth out" and prompt the establishment to alter its thinking about welfare and those who live on it, with it, and in spite of it.

My writing began to attract the attention of assorted types of media. I wrote about single parenthood. I wrote about food stamps. I wrote about housing. I wrote about child support. I wrote about suffering children and unmet needs. I wrote about everything I could, in my attempt to "buck the system" and get those in a position to make change happen, to make change happen.

I began to contact child support advocacy organizations. I researched federal and state laws regarding welfare programs and child support enforcement. I began to send copies of my writing to local, state, and federal legislators. After sending hundreds of copies of my letters, I began to get scattered responses. On February 2, 1995, I went to Capitol Hill, for the second time, to testify about welfare reform and child support issues. Reporter Sandra Evans from the *Washington Post* visited my home the day before the hearings. She wrote a piece about my involvement with welfare programs and child support enforcement, took several pictures of my family, and prepared her story to be printed on the cover of the "Metro Section" the morning of the day I appeared at the Rayburn House Office Building.

When I arrived at the committee's office, several committee members commented to me about the article. When I was riding on the Metro Train, a few passengers recognized me from the papers they were reading. And, when I stopped at a Safeway store for a soda, the cashier told me that she read the article and liked the picture of my family. It was a bit surreal to be recognized from a newspaper picture, but, I knew that my points were being made. People reading the article might not agree with my views and concerns, but, at least, for better or worse, my views and concerns were being put before the public.

I received a telephone call from Chris Core of WMAL Radio in Washington, D.C., inviting me to be a guest on his radio show, *Evening with Chris Core,* that night following the hearings. Any opportunity to speak out on welfare and support matters was an opportunity that I could not refuse. If I could not be a lawyer and represent people involved with welfare and support cases, then I could be a lay advocate and educate the public. I was certain that with education about the realities of family abandonment and "typical" welfare families, the American public would grow less tolerant of adults who desert their children, leaving those children to be raised on public assistance, food stamps, and the resources of others.

Being on the radio was great. Chris Core is a longstanding, well-known radio personality in Washington, D.C. He made me very comfortable on the show. He asked me questions about the *Post* article, the hearings, and my experiences in the system. After we had our conversation on the show, Chris opened up the telephone lines, and I took questions from callers. It was a tremendous opportunity. The radio audience was interested in the topic, and we took calls for about thirty minutes. Chris signed off for the evening, thanked me for coming out to the station, and suggested that my experience of that day on Capitol Hill, and on the radio, might "mushroom" into something more. It did. Other than some short segments on the local news, my participation in the February 2, 1995, *Washington Post* article was my first involvement with serious media. That involvement opened my eyes, and many doors, with regard to the significant impact and power the media has to influence the course of political issues and public policy in the United States today.

After the radio show, I was invited to participate in other media opportunities. The kids and I were featured in a cover article for the *USA Today* newspaper. I was invited to be a guest on MSNBC. The producer for the MSNBC news show sent a limousine for me to ride into the Washington, D.C., studio. I brought Phillip along with me, thinking he might enjoy the experience. I sat for interviews with the *Washington Times, Newsweek, Good Housekeeping,* and *Woman's World* magazines. It was exciting to have the chance to share my information while getting information out to the public. It was disappointing, however, to learn that even though an article is written by a major newspaper or magazine, it may never be read by anyone other than the writer, and perhaps, a first-line editor. That was the case with both *Newsweek* and *Good Housekeeping*. But, it was always better to try and fail, than not to try at all.

I had similar experiences with television media. After writing a piece of poetry entitled, "The Other Side of Welfare," and having it read by several television producers, I was contacted by *Good Morning America,* CNN, *Dateline NBC, CBS Sunday Morning,* the *Oprah Winfrey Show,* D.C.'s own *Broadcast House Live,* and some other local D.C. news shows regarding possible appearances. A *Good Morning America* producer went so far as to discuss New York travel plans with me. But, disappointingly, my story was bumped by some Austrian balloonists, and the kids and I did not make it to New York.

That, I learned, is just the nature of the media. The media can make matters important to the public. The media can cajole legislators and politicians to propose policies that they would never otherwise consider. The media is an important, though fickle, force in societal evolution. It should be respected. It should be feared, at times. And, if it does not care about an important issue, it should be ignored until it sees the light.

Although most of the TV appearances fizzled into vast nothingness, I did have the opportunity to speak several times on the Rush Limbaugh radio program. I have had several pieces of my writing read by Dr. Laura Schlessinger, participated in a nationally broadcast Christian radio program, been a repeated guest on *The Trumbull and Core Show* in Washington, D.C., frequently took calls on WMAL's former *Rita Foley Show,* and was a one-time guest of host Victoria Jones in Washington, D.C.

My media experiences inspired me to continue writing. All throughout the process of completing my master's degree, I continued to write and research. But, our financial situation continued to be dismal. Once the degree program was completed, we would no longer have enough money to meet our daily living expenses. I needed real, full-time work out of the house. Phillip was in second grade, April was in first, Tricia was in kindergarten, Megan was in preschool, and Thomas could be in day care if, I had a job.

After the *Washington Post* article was published, I heard from Eric on sporadic occasions. He continued to work for Food Lion. We received about $750 per month from him in support. The amount never increased, and he never offered more. Birthdays went by with no gifts or cards from him for the kids. Although he always showed up at my house on Christmas Eve, he relied on me to organize Christmas gifts for the children. He played the role of the devoted dad for a couple of hours each Christmas morning and happily took credit for his appearance of yuletide generosity. The kids did not know that he made no effort to participate in their Christmas gifts. But, they didn't need not know that. They could already discern that their dad was not engaged or interested in us.

Several fathers' rights organizations contacted Eric after I was involved in the *Washington Post* article. Eric told me that lawyers from the groups had offered to help him get custody of the children. Those lawyers did not realize that they were wasting their time. Eric didn't want custody of the children. He didn't want the responsibility. Soon thereafter, Eric packed his belongings, drove his car to the auto-train depot, bought a train ticket to Florida, and moved in with his parents who had moved to Ft. Walton Beach. Whenever I asked him for help or asked him how I was supposed take care of the kids with little income and no assistance from him, he simply told me to "get a job." He would say over and over that I "didn't know that it meant to work," and that it "was time for me to get a real job," and that he could not "do everything." Anyway, he was gone. Probably, I thought, for good. For some odd reason, I still loved him after all his terrible treatment of us. It was painful to think of him being gone, but, at the same time, it was a relief.

Eighteen

The Politicians Just Don't Get It

As citizens of the United States, we are privileged to enjoy the freedoms of a representative democracy. As citizens, we are free to participate in matters of government and may, if we choose, engage in the political process. Our political and government leaders propose the rules and draft the laws that shape the nature of our everyday lives.

Generally, the process of our representative government leads to the enactment of reasonable laws and adequate management. However, when politicians are driven by stereotypes, preconceived ideas, and campaign-related legislative obligations, we sometimes end up with poorly constructed laws founded on flimsy facts and weak premises.

Sadly, for the abandoned and deserted children who are the intended beneficiaries of welfare, our political promulgators traditionally follow stereotypical thinking and cater to inaccurate media interpretations when dealing with welfare reform. If our government leaders and nationwide community at large expect to reform welfare from what they think it is to what they think it should be, they must educate themselves as to the realities of the system. They must open their minds.

Political leaders must keep themselves abreast of many issues. As a practical matter, no single legislator can know everything about every issue that might come before him or her. That is to be expected. However, no single legislator should vote on an issue, rule, or law that potentially impacts our most vulnerable citizens without using due diligence to discern the truth underlying the matter.

In the case of welfare and related matters, our legislators have not done sufficient homework to be able to properly and adequately develop a viable solution to the real problem . . . the problem of parents walking away from their kids . . . leaving the government, by default, to provide for them. When attempting to reform "welfare," the president, Congress, and everyone else involved in the debate must address the plain fact that in today's United States of America, the most prosperous, affluent, educated country in the world, we ignore, allow, endorse, and in some instances, even welcome the abandonment of children by parents who should be obligated to take care of them. We, the most prosperous, most wealthy, most educated people on the planet, allow the weakest of us to be deserted and left to live in poverty. Until the focus of welfare reform shifts from looking at the "lazy" welfare mother to demanding accountability from the dad that walked away . . . we will never see the end for the need to have a "safety net," a "safety" network of expensive, bureaucratic, paper-dense, social programs.

The 1996 welfare reform package was designed with the legislative intent that it would "encourage" personal responsibility by "promoting" work. This piece of the package was developed based upon the premise that "no longer" would "ablebodied" adults be allowed to receive welfare "year after year" without working. The "buzz" words heard throughout the national debate on this issue are consistent, predictable, and easy to recognize.

Political pundits and those who make laws have proclaimed that three million families left welfare subsequent to the enactment of the 1996 reform legislation. It is assumed that most of these "people" left welfare for work, however, there have been no concrete methods employed by state governments to assess and follow the tracks of families after they no longer receive a government assistance check. There are no firm statistics to support an assertion that welfare roles have declined because the single parents of children receiving cash aid became ineligible for public assistance due to the fact that they found, obtained, and retained employment. Due to the fact that no studies or reliable statistics exist, only inferences could lead to such a conclusion.

It is highly likely that the 1994 and 1995 heavy pre-welfare reform media barrage created a presumption in many people that public assistance would no longer be available to single parents and their children, or would be available in a limited capacity only. Because of pre-reform presumptions, many extended families opened their doors to single parents and their children, fearing that there would be no other alternative. This reliance on extended family is a positive consequence of the reform effort. With an extended family for emotional support, financial support, and help with child care, a single mother has a better chance to move her family toward self-sufficiency than if she were to remain isolated and alone, living in public housing. Her children, too, would benefit from living in a home with other family members to help alleviate the deficiencies often faced by children with only one adult present in the home.

Federal officials claim that current welfare policies support single parent families. Ironically, the government supports single parent families because one parent has walked away and won't support the family. That same government is, and remains, slow to catch up to the deserting parent, and even slower to hold that parent accountable. When a family seeks public assistance, the head of the household, usually a single mom, must apply with the local social service agency.

The public assistance program was entitled "Aid to Families with Dependent Children," prior to the enactment of the 1996 reform law. Aid to Families with Dependent Children, or AFDC, was a more appropriate name for the program than is its current title, "Temporary Assistance for Needy Families." The AFDC program emerged from the 1964 declared "War on Poverty," led by President Lyndon Baines Johnson, and was intended to protect children, not their parents, from the negative effects of poverty.

Children are the intended recipients and beneficiaries of public welfare. Certainly there exist limited programs that offer short-term financial assistance to disabled and mentally ill adults, however, that type of assistance is not "welfare" as addressed by the federal reform effort. A mother applying for welfare must prove to the state she lives in that she lives with each of the children she claims on her application form. She must prove that the father of her child or children does not live with the family and that she receives no support from him. She must assign all of her rights, and the rights of her children, to seek, obtain, and collect child support from the absent parent over to the state.

A single mother applying for welfare benefits must, literally, make herself and her child or children, financial wards of the state in order to receive the relatively small cash grant provided by the Temporary Assistance for Needy Families program. As I was once rudely informed by the Fairfax County, Virginia, District Office of Child Support Enforcement, "When you applied for welfare, you gave up your rights. If you get a check and sign it, you have no rights." Single parents who apply for and receive welfare payments for their children put themselves at the mercy of state child support and social service bureaucracies.

These parents cannot seek child support from the parent who abandoned them. These parents, by law, must wait for the state to act . . . must wait for the state to establish an order for child support . . . must wait for the state to do its job. For most parents, the wait is long. For some parents, the wait is endless.

I represented a client, Amy, who had two sons, with two different fathers, approximately eight years apart. Both fathers led my client to believe they were interested in getting married. Both fathers alleged that they would help provide and care for their babies. Both fathers told my client that she would not be alone to raise the children. Both fathers left Amy for younger women, women with no children. Both fathers never paid a penny of child support on their own initiative.

My client sought public assistance because she had no other viable alternative at the time. Amy was disabled and could not work at a standard, full-time job. Both fathers had well-paying, stable employment. Both fathers could be easily located. When Amy came to see me, she was receiving public assistance and was angry and frustrated because she knew that child support orders from the two fathers would provide a monthly income for her sons in excess of one thousand dollars.

The welfare grant she received was three hundred and eighty some dollars. Given the choice, who would choose to take support that was almost one-third the amount that could lawfully be sought, paid, and received? Amy wanted more than welfare. She wanted the fathers of her sons to contribute to their needs. Amy wanted her sons to know that their fathers contributed to their needs. The fathers wanted to pretend that she and the boys didn't exist.

We filed petitions for child support and forced the state child support agency to come into her child support cases. We pushed the agency to set up the orders via wage-withholding. Once the child support payments began to flow into the state agency from the men's employers, she discontinued her welfare grant, and now, Amy and the boys receive the support they are lawfully, and rightfully, due. Amy is "off of welfare," not because of welfare reform . . . but because we forced the state child support agency to act.

Expedient child support pursuit by state agencies must be a fundamental component of welfare reform initiatives. In today's economy, it is not fiscally possible for single parent families to move from assistance to actual self-sufficiency without ongoing support and regular contributions from the absent parents. Aggressive, expected, and demanded child support establishment and enforcement are the missing pieces of the federal welfare reform puzzle.

Too many of my clients were in positions just like Amy's. I attempted for almost three years to force my local child support agency to establish and enforce a proper child support order. For three years my kids and I sat on welfare, while my husband freely led the life he desired and paid little, if anything. I, as a welfare client, was powerless to do anything but wait. This scenario is too common. This scenario is at the heart of the ongoing welfare problem. This scenario should not be tolerated, but it is being ignored by local, state, and federal legislators who are in a position to change the system, fix the problem, and really change welfare "as we know it."

That day in May 1992, when I received a letter of encouragement from then President George Bush Sr., I decided to turn the frustration, anger, and worry that occupied my mind day and night since my husband's desertion, into something positive. I decided to share my experiences with people who could impact the system in an effort to improve circumstances for other single parent families like mine. I started to write letters to the editor. I called in to radio talk shows. I contacted my state and local legislators. I organized community forums on child support enforcement and the struggles of attempting to secure support. After several years of trying, I, at last, was offered the opportunity to testify at congressional hearings during the summer of 1994.

During my first two years of amateur advocacy, I collected a sizeable stack of form letter responses. I received responses from members of the U. S. House of Representatives, members of the U.S. Senate, form letters from the Governor of Virginia, my local delegates, and county supervisors. All were form letters except the one from President Bush. I was determined to press on until I actually met with these people. I needed to see them, speak with them, face-to-face. I had to tell them my story so that they could learn about the "other side" of welfare. My side.

The first hearings I participated in were held in July 1994. I prepared two hundred copies of a written statement but was determined to not be another witness who simply reads from a piece of paper without making an impact. I received a parking pass and was allowed to park my car in the Rayburn House parking garage. In order to get my main message out, the message that welfare reform must be grounded on a government demand that parents be accountable to support their children, I had to be a bit creative.

I decided to bring in a copy of the movie *Kramer vs. Kramer* to make my point. The movie, starring Meryl Streep and Dustin Hoffman as two parents entrenched in a brutal custody battle, contained a poignant scene between Hoffman and his movie son, Justin Henry. In the scene, the two were sitting down to an evening meal of salisbury steak TV dinners. After expressing his distaste for the food provided, the little boy got up from the table and proceeded to take a half-gallon of ice cream out of the freezer. Dad immediately asked, "What do you think you're doing?" He received no response, while the little boy continued to scoop ice cream into a bowl.

Dad then began to warn, "Don't you go any further. Don't you do that. Stop it . . . " All to no avail, as the boy raised a spoonful of ice cream, ready to take a bite. The little boy heard his dad's threats, but was not deterred. This analogy is similar to the government's present position of authority when matters of child support are involved. On paper, the law presents an intent to enforce child support orders. In reality, idle threats of incarceration, license suspension, and tax refund intercepts simply do not deter the majority of delinquent, absent parents from avoiding their child support obligations. In reality, a majority refuse to pay, and that same majority proceeds on with life, with no legal consequences to speak of.

I was nervous as I waited in the hearing room for my turn to sit at the witness's table. I had prepared. I was ready. And I was disappointed at the informal nature of the hearing and frustrated that perhaps only one committee member would be sitting to hear my testimony.

After an hour and a half, my name was called. Four members were present. I offered my presentation, listened to two other witnesses offer theirs, and then answered a few questions from the committee members. I left feeling that I had not accomplished much. It was just a procedure. Hearings were scheduled. Hearings were held. But to what end? I don't know. With most committee members not present for most of the testimony, my effort to make my point fell far short of what I had hoped. I left that day determined to try again.

During the days following my appearance, I sent letters to every member of the committee, asking for the opportunity to meet with them to discuss issues of child support and child support enforcement. I called the Washington, D.C., offices of each member to check on the status of my request. I never received a response. I had something important, something relevant to say. My points about child support and the necessity for support to be collected in lieu of public assistance, my presentation about the plain fact that child support collected, dollar-for-dollar, offsets the need and eligibility for welfare payments, seemed to fall on completely deaf ears.

These legislators did not know what they were proposing. They knew nothing about the realities of living on "the system." The only question I was asked by the panel during the hearing was, "Ms. Cave, wouldn't it be easier for you to go to your local welfare office when you have problems getting your check than it would be to come to Capitol Hill?" I had never mentioned having problems getting "my check." My testimony was solely focused on parental accountability. I had no idea what he was talking about. Unfortunately, for all of the abandoned children, parents, and families in the United States, neither did he.

In 1995, President Bill Clinton and congressional leaders came to an "agreement" that welfare benefits failed to help young adults establish economic independence. I was angry when I read about this "agreement." It was obviously devoid of a factual basis. Welfare was not intended to help young adults establish economic independence. The inference that its purpose was confined to pushing adults into economic prosperity is false and unsupported by the law itself.

In 1995, the government went further to assert that reforming welfare would break rising welfare dependency and would return young people, especially parents of young children, to lives of self-reliance and dignity. Again this type of supposition or presumption is based on a faulty premise. Welfare benefits are for dependent children. Welfare benefits are not for adults. Welfare benefits are for kids who are not properly supported by an absent parent.

When will the government acknowledge this fact? When will the government talk about this fact? When will the government educate itself about this fact? When will the government listen to those of us who have lived in a circumstance where we had no choice but to turn to welfare after being deserted by the other parent of our children?

The stated goals of the 1996 welfare reform law included stimulating work, promoting healthy marriages, and reducing nonmarital births. Work requirements were put into place for single mothers with children over the age of eighteen months. Sanctions were imposed upon the families and children of mothers who did not obtain employment within the specified period of time required by the state of jurisdiction. Families were informed that the receipt of benefits would be limited to a total of five years, a warning designed by the government to "make it clear" to recipients that welfare was temporary.

This was all assembled in a "tough love" package of legislation that overwhelmed the national media and reinforced stereotypical ideas of lazy, bob-bon eating welfare moms with twelve children and no source of support, who were an incessant drain on society. Stories of moms buying Twinkies and liquor with food stamps. Stories of women having babies for the sole purpose of generating a monthly welfare check. Stories of drug-addicted mothers filling up all available public housing units. Stories driven by sensationalism, not facts.

The focus of welfare reform was putting single mothers to work. That's it. Plain and simple. In a country where matters involving the safety and well-being of children are supposed to be a top priority, the government plainly and wrongly determined that forcing single mothers into low-paying jobs and forcing their children into low-quality child care would resolve the national welfare problem.

Whereas, in fact what would resolve the problem would be if our government would put into place no-tolerance policies with regard to parents who abandon their children. No longer should it be socially acceptable for a man to run away from his family, for something or someone better. No longer should it be culturally comfortable for a woman or a man to dispose of their first family, their first children, and simply move on for new families and new children without consequences.

In February 1995, I returned to Capitol Hill. This time, I tried to reach the legislators with a presentation that was interactive, as well as creative. The promises of tougher child support enforcement that were being bantered about were nothing more than empty promises. Promises that looked good on paper, sounded good in sound bites, but were, unfortunately, sadly empty.

This time, to make my point, I used sticks of chewing gum. I removed the gum from each wrapper and carefully put the wrappers back together so the gum appeared to be inside. At the beginning of my testimony, I passed what appeared to be a stick of gum out to each of the committee members. During my statement, I described the existing child-support system. I reviewed some of the reform proposals, including alleged enforcement improvements, and then asked the legislators to open the gum.

I made the analogy that the child support provisions in the welfare reform package would in reality, not be effective as inferred. In fact, the provisions in the package fostered an unwarranted complacency that support enforcement would improve. However, like the empty gum wrappers, the promises for improved child support enforcement were empty and unsatisfying.

Almost six years later, welfare numbers are on the rise and child support enforcement sits at a national collection rate of 37 percent, a rate, perhaps, 10 percent higher than the national collection. A 10-percent increase following a monumental legislative reform effort is not a significant success. Federal officials continue to classify child support enforcement as "an important component" of welfare reform. Although it is admitted that child support, for low-income families who receive it, makes up to 26-percent portion of a family's budget, the need for aggressive, reliable, dependable child support enforcement is wrongfully not given the priority and the attention it needs in the welfare reform scenario.

President George W. Bush plans to toughen the 1996 welfare reform legislation that is up for reauthorization during the fall of 2002. In public statements, the president urges Congress to "push more people" from public assistance into work. The president has requested that Congress increase work requirements for single mothers receiving public assistance from thirty hours per week to forty hours per week. Common sense would say that more work, therefore, more income, should be a good thing.

The administration, however, is not using common sense, when it wants to increase work requirements, without increasing funding for the child care necessary for the children of the mothers moving from thirty to forty hours each week. As a practical matter, children of struggling, single mothers, deserted to take care of all their needs on their own will be put at risk of being left improperly or unattended for up to ten hours a week. How can our government force this type of risk on our most vulnerable citizens?

The administration also advocates for programs to strengthen and encourage marriage and promote "responsible" fatherhood.

Although the president's "Blueprint for New Beginnings," his welfare reform overview, concedes that "no law can make people love one another," the administration requests that three hundred million dollars be directed toward efforts to promote marriage and foster responsible fatherhood. This proposal sounds pleasant and proactive; however, throwing money at people will not change their hearts. The president cannot pay fathers to return to their families.

Dr. Wade Horn, assistant secretary of the Department of Health and Human Services, is right when he asserts that, "the absence of fathers from children's lives is a major cause of social problems." As a single mother of five children, I live the consequences of fatherhood abdication every day. As a legal aid lawyer, I attempt to fight for the rights and needs of women and children left behind by men and fathers who decided one day to walk away . . . without consequence . . . looking for something or someone better.

President George W. Bush is right when he asserts that, "work is the pathway to independence and self-respect." However, President Bush is devastatingly wrong when he formulates welfare policies based on stereotypes and the American "idea" of what welfare is really all about. Welfare is about children—children who are not being supported by an absent parent. Welfare payments are not for the adults. Welfare payments are for the children.

A forty-hour-per-week work requirement, without forty-hour-per-week child care assistance is going to result in children of single mothers being left alone while mom fulfills her work requirement. Mom and the children will be put at risk . . . all the while . . . where is Dad? What about a work requirement for an absent dad? How can President Bush push for marriage when so many men choose to abandon their families?

Approximately 70 percent of families currently living in public and assisted housing units are families consisting of single mothers and their children. Generally, these families have pitifully meager incomes due to the easily substantiated fact that many fathers in the United States today affirmatively choose to walk out on their kids . . . leaving single mothers, and by default, the government, to raise them.

Dr. Horn, President Bush, and Health and Human Services Secretary Tommy Thompson recommend public awareness campaigns directed toward responsible fatherhood. Responsible fatherhood would eliminate the need for welfare assistance in most cases. The neediest families in this country today are families living in the aftermath of parental abandonment. It is time for the United States to take a stand against parents who walk out on, or away from, their kids.

In the United States today, a father can move away from his child, jump from state to state, avoid any and all financial responsibility, make a new family, find a new home, live a comfortable life, and never look back . . . all the while, his child and her mother struggle on welfare, hear empty promises from state child support agencies, and end up living in a tent because they have no money for housing. Yes, marriage is preferable. Many of us wish our husbands would be responsible and decent fathers. But, they—not us—make other choices. What solution do Dr. Horn, President Bush, and Secretary Thompson offer us?

Nineteen

What, Exactly, Have You Been Doing All This Time?

I had a bachelor's degree. I had a graduate paralegal certificate. I had been in a legal fellowship program at Georgetown University Law Center. I had a master's degree in management. I had five kids under five, and no job. My resume was chock full of education and community volunteer work. I was qualified. I was overqualified. I sent out hundreds of resumes, but received only one call to interview. I had no experience with computers or office management or accounting. I had been involved in a most challenging type of management, alone, for almost five years. I did not have real world work experience. I was a single mom. That should have qualified me for something, shouldn't it?

I worked as a bank teller. I worked as a preschool teacher. After I was married, I worked in several part-time positions. But, after I had Tricia, and Eric left for the first time, I did not hold a job outside of my home. Taking care of three, and four, and five babies alone seemed like a full-time job in itself. Although I stayed up late every night while I studied and might be able to work at night, as a practical matter, I didn't think I could work all night and still be able to care for the kids adequately during the day. I needed to find a regular, 9-to-5, full-time position, with benefits, good pay, and flexibility. It would be tough to find such a job, but I had to try.

I knew that job discrimination based on familial status is illegal. Technically, an employer could not refuse to hire me because of my being a single mom of five. Technically, an employer who would refuse to hire me for such a reason could be held legally accountable for unlawful discrimination. Even so, I never told a prospective employer of my single parent status.

I applied over and over for jobs listed with the Fairfax County Government. I was on the county's Welfare Reform Task Force. I sat on the Advisory Social Services Board. I participated in county hearings and meetings and public assistance forums, but I never received a call from the county for an interview. I had plenty of education—more, actually, than was required for most of the positions I applied for. However, after more than a year of trying, I had received not one call, not one interview.

Thankfully, a job as the director of children's ministries at my church opened up. The long-time director was retiring, and her position, a full-time, paid position, was available. I applied immediately. Since I had been baby-sitting and teaching Sunday school and running mother's day out programs at the church for several years, I thought I had a good chance to be hired. I prepared a new copy of my resume, borrowed a suit from my sister in California, and could not sleep at all the night before the interview. I had to get the job. My student loans were coming due within months. We had no income other than the $750 per month from Eric, but with him in Florida, out of the jurisdiction of the Virginia courts, that income became tediously unreliable.

I arrived early for the interview. I loved the suit and entered the interview feeling hopeful and upbeat. Present were the church's rector, the former director of children's ministries, a church pastor and member of the staff selection team, and a well-respected member of the church's vestry, who, also happened to be a prominent, Fairfax attorney. I believe I answered the questions well. I knew the church's children's programs inside and out. I had worked with the Sunday school curriculum for several years and was able to clearly articulate to everyone there what my goals would be if I received the opportunity to serve the church and my family, through real, full-time employment.

My hopes were quickly dashed when the former director of children's ministries told me that as a single parent of five, I had too much responsibility at home to have the job. She was kind in her remarks, but serious. I knew I would not be hired. The Fairfax attorney gave me signals, too, that I was not their choice for the job. But, he did more. During his questions for me he stated that he thought I wanted to be a lawyer. I responded that I did, but that it just hadn't worked out and was not meant to be. One week later, I received an acceptance letter from the District of Columbia School of Law.

The D.C. School of Law was formerly known as the Antioch School of Law. Antioch was known for its commitment to public interest law. When the school closed for financial reasons, it was reborn as the D.C. School of Law, a public institution intended to serve the citizens of the District of Columbia by both educating new attorneys and providing free legal services to poor people. I forgot that I had applied. I had filled out the paperwork back in the fall and hadn't given it a second thought.

I called my sister in Los Angeles. I thought that my window of opportunity to go to law school and become a lawyer was closed after the summer of 1992. Here it was, almost four years, one child, and one degree later, and the opportunity was literally sitting in my hands. All I had to do was rearrange my life and the lives of the children, quickly apply for financial aid, and mail in my letter of acceptance. My sister offered to pay the required $300 deposit. I happily marked "yes" on the form and mailed in my response. I was actually going to go to law school.

In an attempt to focus on earning an income and on my need to make enough money to meet our expenses, I had put the thought of law school out of my mind. I was convinced that I had to find a job as soon as possible. Phillip was in third grade, April was in second, Tricia was in first, Megan was in kindergarten, and Thomas was three. My classes began the second week of August. The kids had three weeks to go before their schools were back in session. At first, when thinking about making baby-sitting arrangements for all five kids, all day every day, for three weeks, I panicked. I had to report to class in Washington, D.C., by 9:00 A.M., that first Monday. I had to have my books purchased, my assignments read, and my hands ready to take extensive notes.

I was nervous. I was excited. I was overwhelmed. I felt a bit like I had back in high school on the first day of a new school year. I was afraid to drive downtown by myself. Although I had moved to Northern Virginia in 1980 and was familiar with Washington, D.C., I was not comfortable driving downtown. The last time I drove downtown before starting law school was to take Megan to meet her class for a field trip. Her class was supposed to meet at the Smithsonian Museum of American History at ten in the morning. I brought all the kids with me that day, hoping to impart a little bit of history on each of them. But, thanks to my poor navigational skills, we never made it to the museum.

Late at night, when it was dark and quiet, I got very nervous about getting myself to class on time, downtown, everyday. The nighttime was the worst for worry. The nighttime was the worst for loneliness. But, the nighttime was the only free time I had to work, to read, to write, and to study. In my first-year law student guides, it was repeatedly stated that first-year law students should not work outside of their studies more than twenty hours per week. Being a mom to my kids, keeping the house, doing the laundry, preparing the food, shopping for groceries, attending community meetings, mowing the yard, and taking care of homework, PTA, and school-related matters took up much more than twenty hours per week. As I sat at my kitchen table the first night before class began, my mind filled with doubt.

My financial aid was held up due to a misplaced undergraduate transcript. Although the school would wait on their tuition, my baby-sitters and the metro station manager would not wait for their payment. I used the money I had, our support money from Eric, to pay for my parking and metro fares and baby-sitting. We ate lots of macaroni and cheese and turkey hot dogs. I was grateful to receive school supplies from the Fairfax County Department of Housing's Family Self-Sufficiency Program. School supplies for five children in Fairfax County, Virginia, schools generally cost us about two hundred and fifty dollars each September. Between law school and grade school, with six students in the house and only $750 to cover a month of expenses, financially, things were not promising.

I spent most nights lying half awake, always having an ear open for a restless child, a possible vandal, a problem with the house, or a phone call in the middle of the night related to some new problem with Eric. Even though Eric was in Florida living with his parents and Billy, he would call me, usually in the middle of the night, when he wanted or needed something. Thankfully, because of the distance, there was no way I could feel compelled to help him. He had a way of flip-flopping our situation to make me always question myself and my responses to his requests. Common sense told me that Eric needed to grow up, be responsible, and support his family. My family told me that Eric needed to grow up, be responsible, and support his family. My friends told me that Eric needed to grow up, be responsible, and support his family. Eric told me that I was a nag, that I always belittled him, that I thought he was stupid, and that I never allowed him to do anything with the kids. I knew he was wrong, but I tended to act as if he was right. In doing so, I just enabled him to keep right on keeping me stuck in the same position. I would help him when he would not help us, and when he would not help himself.

The morning finally came. Child care was covered. I had my transportation plan ready to go. I had enough money for the metro, parking, and a day's worth of soda. I got up around 5:30 and was ready to go by 7:00. I left the house at 7:15 and ended up running up the escalator at the Van Ness Metro Station at 8:56 that morning. Four minutes to get to class . . . the first day . . . the first class . . . the first step toward a new life for all of us—and for those I might help in the future.

Twenty

Becoming a Barrister

I did not like lawyers. I never wanted to be a lawyer. After being turned down for help by more than twenty lawyers the evening my husband abandoned us, I liked lawyers even less. Now, I was on the verge of becoming one. One of "them." One of the ones who, frequently, enable absent parents with money to avoid equitably providing for their kids, while leaving the custodial parents with all of the responsibility and insufficient resources to handle that responsibility.

My first class was torts. It began at 9:00 A.M., four mornings per week. I loved sitting in class, asking questions. I enjoyed every moment of class. Our D.C. Law School professors used the Socratic method of teaching, which involves putting students on the spot, asking tough questions, and at times, a bit of embarrassment. The intent of the Socratic method is to get a student used to the "on-the-spot" atmosphere of the courtroom, the pressure of being questioned by a judge, and the reality of having to "think on your feet." Many students were intimidated by the Socratic method. I loved it.

Megan had a difficult time adjusting to kindergarten. After attending several years of preschool at our church, she had to move on to public school. Megan had always enjoyed school. She was sociable, engaged, and friendly at her church school, but for some reason, she had fits of hysteria, that year, when she went to kindergarten at our local public school, Virginia Run Elementary. The school counselors and principal worked extensively with Megan in their attempt to determine why she had such difficulty in adjusting.

On some days, her reactions were so severe that I had to leave school and come home. On other days, I never made it to my first class. Megan's troubles caused me to miss a great deal of my torts class. In the study of law, academic success is usually achieved by performance on one or two exams. As a first year law student, I had mandatory academic requirements, and the passing of certain courses was not optional. To my horror, I failed my first semester of torts. Without a passing grade in torts, I would not graduate from law school and I would lose my financial aid. I was embarrassed and humiliated by the 55 percent I received on my final grade that first semester of torts. I never told anyone about my failure, and again I questioned my determination to become a lawyer and had doubts about my ability to pass the most basic of courses, torts. I took study seminars on torts. I listened to study aid audiotapes on torts. I played the tapes in the car, at home, everywhere I went. I worked very hard to pick up my grade in that class. I had to, and after taking the class twice, I passed.

Phillip, April, Tricia, and Megan went to a wonderful neighbor's home at 7:15 on the mornings I had class at 9:00 A.M. My neighbor Diana walked the kids to the bus stop and saw that they safely made their way to school. After Thomas and I dropped everyone else off, we drove to a local day care center, where Thomas spent his day.

The worst part about my first year law school experience was the effect it had on Thomas. Four days a week, he was in day care from 7:30 A.M. until 6:30 P.M. The center seemed pleasant. The director was nice, and Thomas's first teacher was terrific with kids. The first month went by without incident. When Thanksgiving approached, Thomas began to have troubles at the center. At night, he complained of being hit and bitten by other boys. He also began using words that he did not hear from me or his siblings at home. I spoke with the director at the center and learned that a particular little boy who was at the center all day, every day, had become a serious discipline problem. They were trying to cope with it. I also learned that Thomas's teacher had recently left the center and that a search was on for a replacement. That first year, Thomas must have had six or seven teachers at the center, several of whom could not speak English. Putting Thomas in a child care facility as much as I did that first year was a bad decision. He suffered obvious detrimental effects from the transient nature of his teachers, the discipline problems of other children, and the lack of structure at the center in the afternoons when the regular teachers left for the day and high school girls arrived to supervise. I would never choose to put Thomas in a place like that again. And, I didn't.

During the spring of my first year of law school, Eric returned home. He left his parents home in Florida, returned to Virginia, had a vasectomy, obtained a job with Nabisco, Inc., and promised that he wanted to "work things out" and "make things better." I was dubious about his promises. Historically, such promises from Eric had always fallen completely flat. I was having a rough time handling the rigors of law school, the demands of parenting five children, and the stress of living on little income. The "idea" of having another adult in the house to help me was very appealing. The "idea" of having more income to live on was enticing. The "idea" of being able to engage in an adult relationship again after seven years of being basically alone was comforting. I contacted the department of housing to find out if Eric would be allowed to move home with us under the terms of my housing contract. His income from Nabisco was twenty-seven thousand dollars per year. With a family of seven, we would be allowed to continue under our contract. With that news, Eric moved home.

Things seemed to go well for a while. Eric coached Phillip's softball team. He was available, at times, to pick up Thomas or take the girls to their dance classes. Although he refused to help with household chores, that was a "woman's" job, I was happy to have him there with us and could not bear the thought of his leaving again to leave me alone with the responsibility. Eric did well at Nabisco at first. He earned the privilege of driving a company car and began to coach youth football during the summer of my second year at law school. Eric loved football. After giving up his possibility to play college football to enlist in the Air Force, he continued to long for the opportunity to play. If he could not play, he could coach. Eric was, and is, an excellent football coach.

We argued a lot. He would not pick up after himself. He would not mow the yard without being nagged. He left fingerprints on the walls after reading a newspaper. He did many things to irritate me. But, it was good to have a man in the house. It was good to not be alone. I could deal with sloppiness and laziness and other relatively benign issues. I did not, however, think I could deal with being alone again.

Eric had a bit of advocacy in him, too. We would argue fiercely about our own issues, but, he would seem to have reason when it came to seeing our problems in the context of other people. To that end, we participated in several child support advocacy efforts together. He did a videotape with me about child support enforcement for the "Monitor News Network." He sat for an interview with me for several magazines and agreed to speak with a *USA Today* reporter about our child support experiences. When he talked about child support and parental accountability with regard to other people, or generally, he was objective and fair. When it came to our case, however, he would not accept responsibility.

During the fall of 1997, our daughter April was injured in a school bus accident. One morning, I was paged during class by a paramedic on his way to the hospital with April in the ambulance. Initially I panicked. The paramedic jumped ahead of my panic with his words by letting me know that April was slightly injured in a school bus accident and that they were going to the hospital as a precaution only. Eric was on the road with Nabisco and not available. Being in D.C., I couldn't get to the Fairfax hospital for an hour and a half, so, I called my parents, who could get to the hospital an hour before I could, and they agreed to go. April was treated for a leg injury and left on crutches.

Thankfully, the accident was not serious. Under the circumstances, it could have been. A large dump truck had attempted to pass the kids' full-size Fairfax County Public Schools bus on Pleasant Valley Road, a narrow, winding country-like road that bordered our neighborhood and provided the sole, direct route to the elementary school. When the two vehicles passed, the large mirror on the truck crashed into the side window of the bus, causing glass to fly and the bus to stop abruptly. April's leg was injured due to the jolt that occurred when the bus stopped. At this particular point in the road, the asphalt was not wide enough to accommodate both vehicles. It was obvious that if two such similarly situated vehicles crossed paths again at that spot, the same crash would result. Authorities that were contacted by worried parents did nothing to immediately reduce the risk involved with our school buses and large, commercial trucks daily traveling that narrow road. The road had become a quick and easy cut-through between two major highways. The commercial convenience seemed to outweigh real risk. Several weeks later, my children were again on the bus, this time, coming home from school. Again, the bus collided with a truck at a narrow point in the road. This time, something had to be done.

A group of frustrated and scared neighborhood parents organized a car caravan in protest. I contacted the local news outlets to inform them of our plight. I went to the Fairfax County Board of Supervisors to ask for their help. Parents and children, alike, wrote letters of concern to local newspapers. We were worried. We were scared, and our local delegate called me to say he had "ten trucking lobbyists in his office" and that it would be good to work out a compromise. But, the safety of our children was not open to compromise. On a January morning, ninety-three cars gathered bumper to bumper in front of our neighborhood pool. We followed each other all the way up the road, to the school, through the "Kiss and Ride." I was the school's PTA president at the time. Our principal met me on the sidewalk in front of the building, angry with me that I didn't tell her about our plan. I hadn't told her because we were determined to make a statement, and we didn't want her to try to stop us. We wanted our issue to be noticed. We were on four local television stations that night and made both the *Washington Post* and the *Washington Times,* plus all of our local news papers. If we received no positive help or response from local officials, at least our collective voices had been heard.

My children and I, Eric, and a solid group of Pleasant Valley neighbors traveled to Richmond, Virginia, following our caravan demonstration to speak directly to legislators about the safety of our road and the risk our children faced while being bused to their public school. We spent hours in hearings. Thomas and Megan slept on the floor under our chairs, while I waited for my opportunity to speak. Several parents from our neighborhood testified. We were all very hopeful, but the experience reminded me too much of my experience on Capitol Hill. The legislators appeared to be listening, although, off and on different members would get up, leave the room, return, get up, leave the room, and return again. It was obvious that our issue was not high on anyone's priority list. We did our best. We spoke out. We made our points. But, it appeared that the status quo would prevail. After all, the Virginia trucking lobby was a powerful political force. A small group of impassioned parents were hard pressed to move campaign contribution-dependent bureaucrats.

In desperation, I filed a lawsuit against the Commonwealth of Virginia to force the department of transportation to restrict trucks from using the road. Two weeks after the filing, I filed for an injunction to keep trucks off the road until the case went to trial. The evening before my motion to enjoin was to be heard, I received a telephone call from the attorney general's office. The local attorney was willing to settle the matter through an agreed court order. The Commonwealth was willing to prohibit through trucks on the road until the road could be reconfigured to a size and pattern sufficient to support both commercial trucks and school buses. I accepted the offer, drafted an agreed order, and rested my case. Real parents were able to defeat the bureaucracy while protecting the safety of our children. Our victory in the road matter provides solid evidence of the good the law can do. That victory prompted me to persevere, even though things with Eric were deteriorating.

During the summer of 1998, we moved to a different house in the same neighborhood. My landlord of seven years wanted to sell the house. We were fortunate to find another house to rent in Pleasant Valley. The neighborhood was our home. I couldn't leave it. As far as our housing situation went, we were fortunate to always have a good place in which to live. Eric was great throughout our July 1998 move. He singlehandedly emptied an entire two-car garage full of boxes within two days. I was encouraged and hopeful that moving into the house together had solidified our family unit. Again, he coached football, but this season, I began to notice signs of his involvement with other women.

I found aftershave in his car. I answered telephone calls from women who hung up on me. I found notes in his car or pants that indicated he was involved with someone else. It was all too familiar. I was certain he was involved with someone. Again, perhaps not physically, but he was probably headed in that direction. With a vasectomy, what was to stop him?

Things at the elementary school became strangely odd. I was the PTA president for the second year, and when I attempted to curb spending and reduce the amount of fund-raising the PTA had been doing, I was attacked. I don't know if the attacks were prompted by my media involvement, or my past, or the fact that I was a second-year law student. I don't have any idea why a campaign solidified among an exclusive group of parents to force me out of my position as PTA president. I was libeled. I was slandered. A friend discovered E-mails delivered by several of the parents who were plotting to force me off of the PTA board. And to what end? I do not know. I had already led the PTA for a full year. I attempted to focus on service and charitable efforts and academic basics rather than on fancy computers, flashy amenities, and expensive parties. My ideas were neither appreciated nor accepted by a number of the very well-to-do parents who wanted the PTA to raise thousands of dollars for unnecessary accoutrements.

When I discovered the nature of the effort to force me out of this volunteer position, I became determined to take a stand for volunteers everywhere. I resigned from the PTA and filed a defamation law suit against those persons involved in the campaign against me. I took my case all the way to the U.S. Supreme Court. Unfortunately, the justices declined to grant certiorari in my case. However, the case received substantial local media coverage. *People* magazine called and considered doing a piece on the subject, but, as is often the case with the media, a spicier topic bumped mine from consideration. The case afforded me repeated opportunities to write and speak out about the importance of volunteerism and the value of volunteer work. The foundation of my case was the premise that volunteers should be treated with the same legal protections from common law defamation as persons working in an occupation or profession. Just because volunteers are not paid, they should not receive less than the full benefit of the law while acting in their volunteer capacities. But, when the U.S. Supreme Court effectively said no to my case, I had to put the issue to rest. For a while.

On January 1, 1999, Eric moved out.

Twenty-one

Juvenile Justice

At the D.C. Law School, all students were required to satisfy a requirement of three hundred and fifty hours of clinical assignments for two semesters. Clinical assignments were determined by lottery, and my first one was with the legislative clinic. I spent the semester drafting legislative proposals, researching federal law, and reviewing proposed rules from the *Federal Register*. I enjoy the legislative process. But, three hundred and fifty hours of legislative drafting and review was quite tedious, and downright boring at times.

My second clinical assignment was with the juvenile law clinic. The purpose of the juvenile law clinic was to provide representation to at-risk and underprivileged juveniles in the District of Columbia in matters involving special education, crimes, delinquency, truancy, and neglect. During my first semester in the clinic, I represented a teenage carjacker, a teenage prostitute, and a teenage boy with Down's syndrome. In addition to my poor showing in first semester torts, my compelled participation in this clinic made me nervous and uncertain about my ability to obtain my degree. My clinical supervisor was one of the toughest on staff. Frequently during my tutorials, I would be reduced to tears when she prodded me to take risks and "get out there" and "do my job." I knew that she thought I was afraid, and I was. I wanted, actually needed, to be a lawyer, but, I was scared to death of this clinical requirement.

My job was to keep the teenage carjacker, Anthony, out of jail, to get his immunizations, to get him into school, and to get him into an organized program of supervision and counseling. While I began my case workup and initial planning for the task before me, moment by moment, I had to fight my own resistance to the job. Everything inside me screamed that the safest place for Anthony was in lockup. Not to mention the fact that it was probably safer for the rest of us, too.

Anthony was an almost fifteen-year-old black adolescent. His father lived in a D.C. crack house. His mother had abandoned him and his brother in some woods in North Carolina. Her boyfriend hadn't wanted them around. Anthony and his brother were rescued by their grandmother. The grandmother was a resident of southeast D.C. She had heart difficulties and didn't feel safe with the boys around. But, she had put aside her fears and took the boys in. They had nowhere else to go.

Anthony had been arrested for stealing cars. He and other boys would steal cars and sell the parts to chop shops. Anthony used his share of the money for tennis shoes, cigarettes, and drugs. He often got up before dawn, left the house, walked down the street away from his grandmother's home, smoked weed, and went to class high. Anthony's life was painful, tragic, and full of disappointment. After I went to visit his grandmother's home in southeast, D.C. I decided that I had to do whatever it took to get Anthony connected to something positive.

It was not easy. During my first visit to Anthony's house, he walked me to and from my white, wood-paneled minivan to protect me. On that day, there was an armed robbery at a convenience store on Martin Luther King Boulevard, not too far from Anthony's home. Anthony hung around with other boys who were daily involved with drugs and guns and stealing. When he was arrested on Thanksgiving eve, that year, the officer who pulled him over in a stolen car noticed a firearm in the back seat. Fortunately, the officer knew Anthony and did not fire when he saw the gun.

When I initially met Anthony, he didn't want to go to school. He said that he had only one pair of jeans to wear. I offered to pick up some jeans for him, but when he requested a size thirty-eight waist and appeared to be closer to a size twenty-seven, I opted for sweatpants. He was disappointed, but wore the sweats just the same. He also needed school supplies, so I gathered some from several charitable organizations. And, finally, to get into D.C. Public Schools, he had to have all of his shots up to date.

I sent Anthony and his grandmother to the public health clinic located near their home. The clinic staff would not treat or examine Anthony without a medicaid card, so I sent Anthony and his grandmother to apply for medicaid. They applied but were told that approval might take a while. Anthony needed to get into school immediately. If he was not in school, he was bound to get arrested, or worse. I made an appointment to meet with the school principal. When we met, I explained my job, and she told me what documents I needed to register Anthony for school. I thanked her and promised her Anthony would be back to begin classes within the week.

One afternoon, I met Anthony and his grandmother at their house, so that we could go to the clinic and get the shots taken care of. His grandmother insisted that we drive in her van. Not wanting to appear afraid or rude, I locked my car and followed her to her van. It was obvious that the boys had gotten to the van; the inside was nothing more than a metal shell. All of the upholstery had been stripped from the frame. The springs popped through the seats. The doors were nothing more than metal skeletons. It appeared that the boys had stripped the car of anything that could be sold.

She drove like a maniac, speeding up and down the roads of southeast D.C. We tried several clinics before finding one that might have time to see us. Generally, the lines at clinics queued up outside the door for several city blocks. Most of the lines at the clinics were made up of teenage, or younger, mothers and their children. Many of the children would be crying. The mothers looked frazzled, drawn, and hopeless. The eyes of the children looked longing and empty. Surveying the line at the clinics provided me with a too-honest picture of life on welfare in Washington, D.C. I looked out of place with a briefcase and a suit.

Anthony and I walked into the clinic and got in line. I approached the receptionist, explained who I was, and why we were there. We presented a copy of Anthony's medicaid paperwork and were told to wait in line. Expecting to be faced with the same resistance Anthony's grandmother had faced, I was surprised when the staff agreed so easily to give Anthony his shots. We waited three hours, but Anthony got his shots. I took the immunization record immediately over to the middle school and registered Anthony late that afternoon. He began school the next day. We spent two months going back and forth in front of Judge George Mitchell in the D.C. Superior Court. Anthony often failed to attend school, continued to smoke marijuana, and stole a couple of cars during that time.

Watching the juvenile docket in D.C. Superior Court was a sobering thing. Each morning, a bus carrying juvenile detainees drove to the court from the Oak Hill Juvenile Detection Facility near Laurel, Maryland. Oak Hill was a scary place. Surrounded by barbed wire, high fences, and deserted buildings, the place where delinquent children from the District of Columbia were held looked like a place out of an old, unrated horror movie. I drove to Oak Hill once to visit Anthony. That afternoon, I became determined to get and keep him out of lockup.

Most of the juveniles brought before the D.C. Superior Court were black. Every detainee I saw appeared in court with either a grandmother or a social worker. These boys seemed to have no one to care about them. Judge Mitchell made every effort to give the children that appeared before him opportunities to get their lives straight and to move on to productive adulthood. At the end of my semester, I was able to convince the judge to allow Anthony to move into an alternative school in the District that had twenty-four-hour wraparound services. He could continue his probation, be in school, have a place to live, and, receive a little bit of spending money for his own personal use. I have not seen Anthony since our last day in court.

My second client, Uchenna, was born with Down's syndrome and was an incredibly talented artist. His ability to react to, and use, shapes and colors was amazing. His mother was a tremendous advocate for children with Down's. She worked tirelessly to fight for the needs of her son and other children struggling with the same disability. In Uchenna's case, my job was to require the District of Columbia Public Schools to comply with Uchenna's individualized education plan. Under federal law, a child like Uchenna is entitled to certain services, resources, and educational accommodations. D.C. Public Schools are notorious for ignoring the requirements of the federal law regarding special education. Uchenna's case proved to be no exception.

Through our work at the D.C. Law School, Uchenna received art lessons at Washington, D.C.'s Very Special Arts School. His ability to create and communicate through art was tangible and significant. The education plan put together by the school system contained a provision for Uchenna to receive travel training so he could become capable of getting around the city independently. It also contained a provision requiring that the school system provide Uchenna with a computer to use during his class lessons. Uchenna could learn and communicate at almost an age-appropriate grade level while using a computer with a color monitor. D.C. Public Schools' response to the requirement was to place an old, broken 386 computer unit at the school site. Even if it worked, a 386 model would not be able to use the software programs necessary for Uchenna's educational plan. It was incredibly frustrating. Uchenna wanted so much to learn and be like other kids. The failure of the school system to give him what he was educationally entitled to was unlawful. The formal hearing process for matters in the D.C. Public Schools frequently carries on for months. As a one-semester clinical student, I didn't have months to wait. I filed appeals against the school system. Thankfully, through the resources of a nonprofit, welfare-to-work-type program I was a part of, Uchenna was given a new, Toshiba laptop computer with access to all of the software he needed. My experiences with the D.C. Public Schools helped me to appreciate the education I had received and made me enormously thankful that none of my five children have needs requiring special education services. Parents of special needs children must take extraordinary steps to advocate for their children and must be aggressive in their efforts to require our public schools to provide the resources they are lawfully entitled to.

My third client, Takia, was an incredibly talented singer. Her voice was fabulous. Through our work at D.C. Law School, we helped her to be admitted to an in-patient psychiatric hospital for adolescents in the District. Having a bed in the hospital got Takia off the streets and into school. Her mother was on and off public assistance. Her brother had molested her. Her father was locked up for murder. Takia spent several years running on the streets of the city to support herself. After several suicide attempts, her case came to the law school. I would visit Takia at the hospital at least once each week. During a program put on by the patients, I heard her amazing voice. Her voice was rich and full and gospel-like. When she sang "Eye on the Sparrow," even the most hardened of patients seemed to be touched. Takia needed to develop a reason for being. Through a scholarship at the Duke Ellington School for the Arts and a hospital pass for lesson attendance, Takia began taking voice lessons at the Duke Ellington School. When I last visited Takia at the hospital, she was working on a plan to leave the hospital and perhaps take on a professional singing opportunity.

These three children were presented with enormous obstacles to overcome in their young lives. Takia and Anthony were products of the "system," with parents on, or formally on, welfare, and with little or no hope for the future. Uchenna had a wonderful set of parents with limited resources. Uchenna's geographical location dictated that his educational needs would go underserved and almost ignored. So many of the young people of the District of Columbia-come from underprivileged, sad, and violent backgrounds. It is enormously important that our public schools and local governments work together to protect our children that are considered less than important by the parents that created them. Drugs, violence, and years living on welfare alone are ingredients that promote, provoke, and preserve poverty and hopelessness. With the law, some ingenuity, some advocacy, and aggressive persistence, lives like Anthony's, Takia's, and Uchenna's can be changed forever. It was my privilege to have a part in that as a student at the D.C. School of Law. My experience inspired me, committed me, and motivates me to keep on pursuing justice for children—those most innocent, yet most injured by the irresponsibility of adults.

Twenty-two

The Third Time's the Charm

I never wanted to be a lawyer. My sister, Patti, went straight from college to law school at the University of Virginia. Three days before her graduation from law school, my husband walked out. Some thirty court appearances later, I decided I needed to go to law school to make some kind of difference in a screwed up system that favored deserters and left children in poverty. Although my anorexia and my inability to take control of the disease left me with a less than stellar undergraduate record, I was determined to go to law school. I had to be accepted somewhere. I had to pass the bar, sometime. I had to get the chance to practice and to, finally, make some sort of difference. If I couldn't do it for my own case, I could do it for others.

After I made it through my law school clinics and a successful repeat of torts class, I was in the homestretch of my third year, at last, a few months and a bar exam away from being a lawyer. There were a few snafus and unexpected interruptions that occurred during those last few weeks. Most of them were related to, or involved, Eric. He showed up every now and then to ask for money or to attend a football game. When things were going OK for him, we hardly saw or heard from him. When he needed something or had some type of problem, he would call constantly.

On the eve of the due date for my twenty-five-page legal research paper, Eric insisted on using my computer at a moment I stepped away from it. I asked him not to touch it. I knew he wanted to use the Internet. He said that he just wanted to check the baseball scores, but, I had a bad feeling. My intuition about Eric and his mishaps has always been right. Whether it was knowing that he was involved with someone or figuring out that he had lost his job and wouldn't tell me, I always got a "feeling" when things with him had gone astray.

A significant research paper was a requirement for graduation at D.C. Law School. My paper was about child support enforcement in Virginia. I had written thirty-four pages, with fifty-six footnotes, and was almost finished. I needed to proofread the paper and assemble my bibliography. My timing was not good. Eric was over, and I had to take the girls to softball. When I returned from dropping the girls off at practice, I sat down at the computer, tried to pull up my paper, and was horrified to discover that my entire paper was gone.

I had to go back to the softball fields to pick up the girls, and when I returned home, I had to spend all night reconstructing my paper. Fortunately, I had notes and an outline to work from, but the task was daunting. I had to have the paper ready to submit to my professor the next day. After getting the kids ready for bed, putting in a load of laundry, letting the cat out, and cleaning up the kitchen, I got to work. I wrote all night. It was hard to reconstruct the entire paper overnight. I had worked on it all semester. The thought of losing the entire paper into the unknown abyss of my C drive was a recurring nightmare during my last few weeks of law school. I am not very computer literate. I can use the computer to write, but, I make a lot of mistakes when I try to access unfamiliar features. My nightmare had become my reality. I wrote all night without interruption and turned the paper in on time the next morning. Eric said that he was sorry, but that he hadn't done anything wrong. That was the same mantra I heard from Eric about everything—from leaving us to losing a job—I really wanted to believe him. I really wanted him to change. I waited a lot of years for him to change, but it didn't happen.

My last set of final exams came and went with not too much anguish. Graduation was set to be a three-or-four-hour event. I was happy to graduate, although graduation meant the onset of my student loan repayment. Plus, I really wouldn't be a lawyer until I passed the bar exam. I was enrolled in a bar review course. A bar review course, students would joke, is what really taught the law. Without a bar review course, many law school graduates do not pass the bar.

I thought I was ready to take the 1999 Virginia Bar Exam, which was given in Roanoke at the local civic center. I stayed at a small Holiday Inn in Salem, Virginia. The kids went to California for ten days with my mom. My sister arranged for the trip so that I could have time to prepare and travel without distraction or worry. She was so great with the kids. Patti really tried to give me the resources and time I needed to pass the bar exam. She gave me tips on the exam, and she stood by me with help whenever I needed it.

After the exam was over, I had a three-month wait for the results. Our income was limited to the child support we received through Eric's job at Nabisco. The student loan funds were depleted, and we needed some income right away. The kids loved to spend time at our neighborhood pool during the summer. Located at the end of our street, our community pool became a second home for us during the long days of summer. One afternoon when leaving the pool house, I noticed a flyer advertising for lifeguards. According to the ad, training was provided. Thomas told me that I should be a lifeguard, and at first, I laughed off the idea. It would be ridiculous for me to be a lifeguard. As a teenager, I had taught swimming lessons, but I had not been lifeguard certified.

I thought about the idea a bit more and called the pool manager. At seven dollars an hour, lifeguarding was no high-paying job. But, I could work close enough to home so that day care wouldn't be an issue. I registered for a training class, suited up, and headed to a pool in Annandale, Virginia. The toughest part of the certification process for me was holding my breath. The class was full of youngsters, kids age fifteen to eighteen. Being almost twice their age, I felt a bit out of place. However, everyone was kind and seemed to tolerate me, even when I struggled with my first deep-water rescue attempt. I passed the course and spent the remainder of the summer at the pool.

I obtained a job as a law clerk at a small Fairfax law firm. My boss, Bob, a very experienced attorney and Georgetown Law School graduate, hired me on the assumption that I would pass the bar exam and become an associate with his small firm. Bob and I had philosophies that clashed. My bent toward helping poor people would frustrate him. He wanted to make money, and of course, he needed to keep his firm afloat and make a decent living. Often, Bob would tell me he thought I wanted "to save the world" or work for "goats and chickens." I can't work for goats and chickens, but I do have a heart for people who can't afford high-dollar attorneys when they really need one, especially in cases of family abandonment. It seems inherently unfair to me that citizens who are lawfully entitled to the protection of the law in circumstances of hardship, due to no fault of their own, must pay to access that protection by hiring a lawyer. Too many lawyers take advantage of vulnerable people. Too many people pay too much to lawyers. I did not, and will not, be a part of that ongoing trend.

Working for Bob, I made five hundred dollars per week. Having a monthly income of more than two thousand dollars felt like we were rich. We had money to buy groceries without having to worry about the water or light bill. Although the income was still low, much below the federal poverty level for a family of six, with our housing assistance, we were okay. I learned so much working for Bob. He threw me "out there," so to speak, to learn how to handle different legal assignments. His property settlement agreements were "rock solid," as he put it. His wills and other formal documents were excellent. He was precise in his method and taught me well.

Bob used to tell me that I thought too much "like a client." I would argue back that I certainly didn't think like a client, but that I could understand what a client is dealing with, how fearful a client might be, and that the practice of law should be about more than a billable hour. It should be about protecting and preserving the rights of someone needing legal relief. I will never forget the feeling in my stomach the morning I went to the office and Bob had the bar exam results pulled up on his computer screen. The results were listed by exam number only. I was terrified to look at my results. I got sick to my stomach and threw up in the bathroom a few times. I just couldn't bring myself to look at that screen. Not once—all day.

The word among examinees was that if you received a regular sized, business envelope in the mail, you had passed. If you received a long fabric envelope, you had failed, and the Board of Bar Examiners was sending along a new application. When I finally got the nerve to open my mailbox, I saw a long, fabric envelope. I had failed. My heart sank. What now?

My next task was giving my family and Bob the bad news. I was so disappointed. I felt like my life was over. I had only felt that way two times in my life before that I could remember. Once, when I had to move from Chicago to Virginia between my sophomore and junior years of high school, and a second time when I thought about gaining weight while recovering from anorexia. I didn't know what I would do. My loans . . . my job . . . my finances . . . my kids . . . my obligations. All of my hopes were shattered by the news that came in that envelope.

I was relieved by the response I got with regard to my disappointing performance on the bar exam. My dad offered to pay for me to try again, my sister encouraged me to try again, and Bob was willing to wait for me to try again before firing me. I spent the next four months working and attempting to study. I thought that I could successfully combine both work and study time by learning as much as I could through the tasks Bob assigned. I read the code voraciously. I studied the local and state court rules, and spent hours drafting documents and reading cases. Between the kids and my job, there was no time for a bar review course. Since the review course didn't help me pass the first time around, I wasn't overly concerned about missing the course the second time.

February 2000 came more quickly than I liked. I took Phillip with me to Norfolk, Virginia, for the winter exam administration. Although the material was familiar, I didn't have much confidence about passing. On the drive home from the winter exam, my stomach felt queasy and out of sorts. My intuition was that try two was not good enough to pass either. Although I had a feeling of dread about the results of that second exam, I couldn't focus on it. I had another three months to wait for the results. I would have a job with Bob, at least until then. I had to keep going and, hoping for the best.

The three months passed quickly. The results were released. I received another large fabric envelope. Bob fired me. I was devastated. Two failures. No job. My dad and my sister, once again, offered to pay for and help me try again. From May 2000 through July 2000, my main focus, other than taking care of the kids, was to study. I worked at the pool so that I could earn some money. I studied at every available moment and went to every single bar review class. To fail twice was awful. To fail three times was unthinkable. I couldn't fail again. I was on a mission to pass that exam.

The summer passed uneventfully. No disasters occurred to speak of. The kids went off to camp. I went down to Roanoke to sit for the July 2000 exam. After the exam, as I drove up Interstate 81 out of the mountains, I had a good feeling about the pending results. Of course I could not be certain, but after three attempts, I thought the odds were in my favor. I finished out the summer working at the pool and looking for a job.

I applied for two public services positions during August 2000. Realizing that my law school credentials were not worthy of a high-dollar law firm, and knowing that a money-driven practice was not for me, I sought to find a position with legal aid, as my first choice, or the public defender's office, as my second choice. Prior to the release of my exam results. I interviewed for both positions. Right up front, I addressed my history of bar exam failure. It was embarrassing, but I figured it was better to put it on the table immediately. Since I had failed the exam twice anyone had to look at my ability to pass it the third time a little dubiously. I understood that and didn't expect to be hired for a legal job until after my results were out. Legal Services of Northern Virginia would offer me the opportunity to practice the type of law that I wanted to. I would be able to help other abandoned parents and would truly have the opportunity to improve the standard of living and quality of life for as many children and families as my caseload could accommodate. The opportunity was like a dream come true. Although legal aid new attorney positions involve relatively low salaries, $33,675 in Northern Virginia, I could continue to receive housing assistance. My income as a Legal Services staff attorney would be low enough for my family to remain qualified. In addition, I had a passion for the work accomplished by legal aid organizations. Being allowed to work a case and pursue support and custody orders for parents who have been abandoned and left with inadequate resources, or wives who have been abused, or elderly folks who have been taken advantage of, would be a privilege and at the same time, an awesome responsibility. I was eager for the chance. I prayed to get it.

My interview with the local public defender's office was not all that encouraging. Again, I informed my interviewers about my bar exam difficulties. Of course, I knew that a public defender's job was to defend the accused party in a criminal matter. It is the most basic of premises in our legal system that a citizen accused of a crime must have access to legal representation to adequately preserve their constitutional rights. But, I wrongly assumed that I would get to be a zealous advocate for the wrongly accused. During the interview, one of the attorneys present sharply informed me that 98 percent of my clients would likely be guilty of the crimes for which they had been accused. That would be a problem. The interview ended there.

October 6, 2000, approached quickly. This time, to avoid my gut-wrenching inability to look at the bar exam results on the computer. I gave both my sister, Patti, and my dad my exam number, so that they could look on the Internet and find out for themselves the good or the bad news. Considering all they had done to help me, I felt they were entitled to know as soon as I did. The results were scheduled to be posted at seven o'clock that evening. After school that Friday afternoon, I got a call from Patti, who was in Los Angeles. She asked how I was (it was the "big day" for the third time), and then, quickly, she told me I had passed. Out of the blue. I wasn't expecting that news at that particular moment. After all, the results weren't due out for several hours. Yet, for some unknown reason, Patti had been able to pull up the results in California three hours before I could do the same in Virginia.

I was offered a staff attorney position at Legal Services of Northern Virginia on October 9, 2000. I accepted immediately and began work on Monday, October 16, 2000. I love my work at legal aid. I continue to write editorials about children and the law, families, child support, and other matters involving advocacy for families and children in need. I have had the opportunity to help moms just like me and children just like mine. It is the most amazing thing to me. When I look back at May 16, 1990, the day Eric left for the first time, I cannot really fathom what has occurred and developed in my life and in the lives of my children since then. I am privileged and blessed to do the work I do. The challenge of going up against some of the best, well-paid attorneys in my area, and fighting for the truest of underdogs and winning, is incredible! I am thankful. And, I encourage anyone who experience anything similar to what I have during the ten or so years described in this book, to never say never. Never doubt yourself. Never doubt the motivation that exists in the longing eyes of your children. Never doubt the value of struggling for a higher purpose. Great things can happen. And, they will, with faith, perseverance, and living to put the children first.

Twenty-three

Glimpses of Single Parents

During the years since Eric left in May 1990, I have been fortunate to meet and commiserate with a number of single parents who were left struggling in the aftermath of a family breakup. Some of the the parents were married. Some were not. Some are women. Some are men. Some are very young. Some are not too old. But, all have one important characteristic in common. All are raising a child or children alone.

"Sandy"

Sandy was an unwanted, female baby born in an often treacherous homeland. Life in Thailand was not kind to Sandy. She was rescued from possible death by her grandmother and found herself living on the streets by the age of sixteen. Sandy survived by becoming a loan shark. By necessity, she lived a life of danger and risk taking. But, it was not until she married an American man and moved to the United States that she encountered the most threatening dangers of all.

Sandy was the victim of years of domestic abuse. Her husband earned a decent income, while Sandy stayed at home to care for their young daughter, Victoria. Sandy was beaten by her husband repeatedly, several times to the brink of death. Sandy gathered her courage and left her husband. She and Victoria were the recipients of welfare, food stamps, and public housing in order to survive in an economy that was unfamiliar to Sandy.

Sandy obtained legal counsel to represent her in a divorce proceeding. Having a business and not a domestic law background, her lawyer's work did not result in an optimum outcome for Sandy, or her young daughter. Sandy was left with a large amount of marital debt to pay. She was also left sharing physical custody of Victoria pursuant to an every other week, rotating schedule. Victoria was with Sandy one week and with her father the next week. When Victoria was approximately eight years old, she was molested by a roommate of her father's. Sandy was mortified, sought immediate counseling for Victoria, and pursued the matter legally against the man, and her ex-husband.

Sandy and I researched the law and developed a plan for her to obtain primary physical custody of Victoria. Appearing in court on her own behalf, Sandy represented herself and her daughter's best interests well. After several hearings, she was awarded full physical custody of Victoria. Sandy and Victoria went through difficult times together. When no child support was forthcoming, they relied on public assistance and lived in a public housing complex. Holidays were especially lean, but Sandy worked very hard to build a better life for herself and her daughter.

Sandy earned an undergraduate degree while raising Victoria and living on welfare. She saved every penny, cut corners wherever she could, and struggled to provide Victoria with food, clothing, and daily necessities. As she grew, Victoria struggled with the ongoing effects she suffered from the molestation inflicted upon her at the tender age of eight. Victoria became combative with her mother. The tension escalated to the point that Victoria assaulted Sandy, pushing her against a wall and later, holding her down in the snow on their neighborhood parking lot.

It took several years after the assault for Sandy and Victoria to rebuild a relationship with each other. As is often the case in circumstances where a single mother attempts to provide everything for her child or children, Victoria went without a lot of the "things" she would have liked. Sandy did her very best to overcome significant odds and fought her ex-husband, who had a powerful and well-paid attorney, for custody of Victoria. Sandy's story is similar to that of many women who live in abusive marriages, leave for reasons of safety and security, and must turn to public assistance to survive.

"Diana"

Diana, like Sandy, was involved in an abusive marriage. Her husband, George, attempted to kill her in front of their young daughter. Diana, too, fled the marital home for both her safety and the safety of her three children. They went to court, obtained a divorce, and George quickly disappeared. With no other viable alternative at the time, Diana sought public assistance to provide for her children. The children were stair steps in age, and day care cost more per week than Diana could earn at a minimum wage job, so welfare seemed like the only option. George was ordered to pay child support to Diana for the family. Instead of paying support, he fled to Israel.

Diana went through Virginia's Division of Child Support Enforcement for assistance in collecting her support. She called, wrote, called, visited the office, called her local officials, wrote some more, and did everything she reasonably could to seek out help from Child Support Enforcement. No matter what effort she made, her case sat stagnant for years. George returned from Israel but traveled around the country and continued his record of nonpayment. Eventually, the amount he owed became so high that he was placed on Fairfax County's "Most Wanted" list for child support offenders. After years of trying to locate him, Diana found him over the Internet.

With creativity, ingenuity, and determination, Diana worked with a Virginia U.S. attorney until the federal government caught up with George, tried him, and convicted him for failing to support his children. George spent several years in federal prison. Once released, he petitioned the local court to reduce his child support obligation. He appeared in court, asking the judge to decrease the amount he was paying, asserting that his incarceration hindered his ability to earn sufficient income to meet the terms of the order.

George owed more than $100,000 in child support to his three children. He owed that much before being jailed, he owed that much upon his release, and he continues to owe that much. Thankfully, the judge who heard George's case declined to reduce his support pursuant to George's claim that his income was insufficient to meet his obligation. The judge stated that she would not reduce his child support, since his incarceration had been the result of his own neglect. Unfortunately, the judge did reduce the support order slightly, because Diana's income had increased substantially. During the time subsequent to her divorce, Diana attended and graduated from college, obtained an excellent job, and works hard, every day, to do the very best for her children.

"Jenny"

Jenny and I were the same age. We met at church. We both married young and had unrealistic ideas about our husbands, our futures, and society in general. As young deserted mothers of multiple toddlers, we shared the frustration of living on welfare, the pain of being abandoned by womanizing husbands, the loneliness of parenting without a partner. We each also had parents who walked the fine line between wanting to help their grown child and wanting to take charge and say, "I told you so."

Jenny had discovered she was pregnant while she was still in high school. She married her high school sweetheart, Mark, and hoped for a happy life. Mark, on the other hand, stayed involved with other women and was irresponsible and undaunted by his obligations to be a husband and father. Jenny found herself alone with a preschool-age daughter, a two-year-old son, and an infant. She moved to Virginia from North Carolina so that she and the children could live with her parents. Jenny prayed and hoped that her marriage might be healed, but when she discovered that Mark had had a baby with another woman subsequent to Jenny's moving to Virginia, she knew the marriage was over.

Jenny obtained proper court orders for child support, but Mark ignored them. Having three small children to feed led Jenny to social services to apply for public assistance, while the Commonwealth of Virginia attempted to contact the State of North Carolina about Jenny's unpaid child support. The alleged attempts resulted in nothing, which was the amount of child support Mark paid—nothing.

Jenny and the children eventually moved with her parents to a farm in Ohio. Jenny's hope was to obtain housing separate from her parents so that she and the kids could have a home of their own. She became a paralegal by completing a college degree program and found a well-paying job at a local law firm. Jenny was finally able to move out of her parents' home and into a home of her own. Jenny worked tirelessly to meet her goal and did it with no support, assistance, or concern from the father of her three children. Mark does not see his children.

"Tammy"

Tammy was sixteen when she gave birth to Joey. Joey's dad was generally nonexistent. After Joey, came Matthew and Jonathan. Although the two younger boys had a relationship with their father, it was limited and not productive. Tammy had a history of being involved with abusive men. When we met, she was pregnant with William, baby number four, dad number three. She was living in subsidized housing, receiving public assistance, and searching for a way out, and a way up for her children. Tammy baby-sat at a church where I taught aerobics several mornings a week. We connected immediately because of our common bond—we were both "on the system." We were both hoping and praying for a better future.

When Tammy went into labor with William, my daughters and I took her to the hospital. Her family didn't live close by. Without help from William's father, Tammy was on her own to develop a plan to provide for the boys' food, clothing, shelter, and future. An unexpected obstacle arose when William was diagnosed as almost 100-percent deaf. To find adequate care for William's hearing problem, Tammy researched the problem and fought with Medicaid to get William the help he needed. William was taught sign language, and Tammy developed an interest in medical science.

Tammy obtained a car through a ministry in our local area. Being without an automobile had been difficult for her, but once she had reliable transportation, Tammy's opportunities became vast and open-ended. She enrolled in an training program at the local community college to become an ultrasound technician. Tammy studied, took William to speech training and sign language classes, cared for the boys, worked part time, and passed her course work successfully.

"Paul"

Paul was a forty-year-old single dad. After some ten years of marriage, his wife, Anne, walked out, leaving Paul to be "Mr. Mom" to their young son, Thomas. Paul was devastated and sank into a serious depression. With an almost one hundred-thousand-dollar-per-year income, Anne could afford to pay the expenses on both the marital home and her new place, but after a year or so, and once Paul petitioned the court for support and custody of Thomas, the gloves came off.

As is often the case, once a party hires an attorney and begins to accrue significant legal bills, the tension in a family law case rises to an intolerable level. Paul and Anne had a schedule of visitation set up, where Anne would visit with Thomas several evenings a week for dinner. In addition, Anne would keep Thomas a couple of weekends each month. As time went on, Anne got tired of paying all the bills and told Paul that she was going to decrease the amount of money she was providing to him to cover the household expenses. Once Paul's petitions were filed and set to be heard, Anne hired an attorney and filed for divorce.

Armed with information provided by the attorney about shared custody guidelines, Anne began to whittle away at Paul's schedule with Thomas by asking for more time with him, not for the purpose of increasing her time with her son, but for the purpose of accumulating enough contact hours with Thomas that her support obligation to Paul would decrease. It is this kind of legal posturing and maneuvering that often obliterates what, if any, civil relationship a couple might have left after enduring the breakdown or breakup of their family. Hopefully, in the case of Paul and Thomas, common sense will prevail, and Anne and Paul will work their situation out in a manner consistent with the best interests of their little boy.

"Liz"

Liz and her husband, Charlie, separated in September. They agreed that their baby daughter, Joanie, would stay with Liz and that Charlie would visit with Joanie every other weekend. This arrangement went along for several months, until one evening in January, when Charlie decided not to return Joanie to her mother. Liz fought for eight months to recover custody of her young daughter. During that time, Charlie hired an aggressive lawyer and would only allow Liz to see her baby for one hour at a time in his home. Although the situation was a nightmare, Liz had to see Joanie and went along with Charlie until a proper court hearing could be held.

The court entered an order allowing Liz more time with Joanie, pending a final court date. The trial was long and distasteful. At the end of the day, the judge ordered that both parents share equal time with Joanie. Two days later, Charlie left his job. Two months later, Charlie left the state. After putting Liz through the emotional turmoil of being without her daughter for eight months, Charlie casually "changed his mind" and decided to move to Ohio to pursue a new career—without Joanie. Charlie told Liz that he wants his visitation with Joanie to be "open-ended." Liz believes that Charlie will never see Joanie again.

"Christina"

Christina called me out of the blue. I was washing dishes and yelling at my kids to clean up the house when I answered her call. She was in a panic. Her ten-year-old son had left home earlier that day, and she had no idea where he was. Her sixteen-year-old son, she knew, was using crack cocaine, a habit he had learned from his dad, a prominent northern Virginia attorney. The family had plenty of money, it appeared from the outside, and was well to do with few, if any, problems. Christina's call to me (a former welfare mom) for help was a profound and powerful jolt of societal reality. Family abandonment and desertion were not limited to the poor and uneducated. Family breakdown strikes all types of families. It's damage spans across all classes of society.

Christina told me that her husband came around the house during the day, but spent every night away from home. She was concerned for the children's safety and was fearful about any exposure the kids might have had to her husband's drug habit. She insisted that he was quite blatant about the drug use and that her husband was abusive toward the boys. I suggested that she immediately call the local child protective services or go to a local magistrate to obtain a protective order for her and her sons. I wished her well and encouraged her to seek other resources by providing her with contact telephone numbers. When I hung up the phone, my instinct told me that Christina wouldn't do anything. She would likely remain in the status quo of an abusive marriage for the purpose of retaining access to her husband's income.

"Amanda"

Amanda's case is the one that has touched me the most, thus far, in my practice of family law. Amanda is a single mother of five and is a struggling college student. Amanda is bright, motivated, and cares about nothing more in the world than the well-being of her children. I defended Amanda in two separate custody cases, against two separate fathers. The fathers claimed Amanda neglected her children, provided inadequate supervision, and lacked adequate resources to care for the children, in addition to throwing every other possible allegation at her to see what, if anything, would stick.

Amanda worked very hard to support her children, keep a job, and pursue a college education. She and the children were on public assistance for a short period of time. They had a federal housing voucher and were able to find a nice town home to rent. Amanda made certain that the kids played sports, participated in music, and attended to their homework. She was definitely stretched thin, but she handled it with grace and a smile.

During the first custody trial, we endured a full day of baseless accusations being made against Amanda by the father of her third child, Sarah. He accused Amanda of everything from allowing her six-year-old son, James, to walk around unattended on a busy, four-lane road, to having him go to school without underwear on.

The claims were not supported by evidence, and at the conclusion of the trial, the opposing attorney's strongest argument was that Amanda was an unfit parent because she was a single mother of five, living in Section VIII, federally subsidized housing. "After all," counsel said, "someone who has to turn to public assistance to take care of her children is not a fit parent for those children."

I was floored and offended by his closing argument. I held my composure as I rose to present my closing. After my recap of the facts and a statement regarding the weak character of counsel's evidence, I proceeded to tell the court that there is no legal authority, anywhere, asserting that a single mother of five children, living in federally subsidized housing is an unfit parent for her children. If that were the case, I would not have my children with me.

The judge conceded that there was in fact no legal authority to support the notion that being a single mother of five young children while living in federally subsidized housing is sufficient to warrant a change in physical custody of a child who had been with a parent for her entire life. However, even though there was no legal authority for the change, the judge ordered a change of custody, nevertheless. Sarah will remain with her mother while the case is on appeal. Amanda's case is sadly indicative of the stereotyping and general assumptions that often play a part in decision making when families receiving state or federal aid are involved. It is the kind of stereotyping and assumption making that can rip already struggling families apart. And, it often does.

"Emily"

Emily's story is profoundly sad. Emily was only sixteen when she gave birth to Emma. Emma's father paid little attention to the baby, or to her mother. He was involved with other women when Emma was born. Emily was left to seek public assistance to care for her baby, while she was a baby herself. Emily began to pursue child support for her daughter even before she was born, and learned, firsthand, of the frustrating and forbidding paperwork that infiltrates the process of seeking child support and public assistance. The process was even more daunting for Emily than for most single parents, because she can't read.

Over the course of eight years, Emily and Emma moved from nanny job to nanny job, trying to combine employment with a place to live. Emily worked to be certain that Emma went to good schools, studied hard, and had opportunities to be involved in extracurricular activities. When Emily was employed, she and Sarah were safe and comfortable; when she was not, they lived in a tent located in a secluded park area. Emily finally obtained a child support order after nine years of pursuing Emma's father. Although an obligation was established, the judge denied Emily's request to make the order retroactive to the date she had first applied for support, because Emily's father had moved through several states, never remaining in one state long enough for a court to obtain legal jurisdiction over him.

Twenty-four

And Justice for All?

In our American society, we pride ourselves on our long-established system of civil and criminal justice. Unfortunately, as time has evolved, family breakdown has become an increasing occurrence in the United States. A clear one-third or more of the family units in our country today are headed by single parents. In the competitive and sometimes harsh American economy, single parents frequently have trouble making ends meet. Generally, the law of land, across all states, is that children are entitled to receive the benefit and support of both parents, whenever and wherever possible.

The sad reality is that too many children go to sleep every night in broken homes, without enough money for food, have heat, or receive adequate medical care. Often, the reason for this poverty can be traced directly to the breakup of a family, the desertion of a parent, or the birth of a baby to an unwed teenager. It is one thing for the adults of this country to make choices that are detrimental to their own best interests. It is entirely another, and a wrong thing, for the adults of this country to make choices that are detrimental to the best interests of their children.

Our children are the most valuable resource we have as a nation. Raising responsible, accountable, and productive citizens is the best thing we can pursue as a country to ensure a bright future for all of us. To allow our children to suffer at the hands of a justice system that favors those with money while leaving those without behind, is contrary to the principles on which the United

States was founded. Our system, our collective attitude, and our people must take a stand against parents who desert their children, leaving those children to be raised on and by the resources of our government.

Epilogue

Twice, I was asked by the "Dr. Laura" radio talk show to participate as a guest in a radio segment with Deputy Secretary of Health and Human Services, Dr. Wade Horn. Twice, I prepared, rearranged my work schedule, and made every effort to be informed, knowledgeable, and ready to ask Dr. Horn my questions about fathers who desert their families and suffer few if any consequences. Twice, my interview was cancelled. Dr. Horn, however, did go on, while I lost out on a rare opportunity to present the Bush Administration with a perspective on welfare reform that it either hasn't, or won't, acknowledge.

The fact that Dr. Horn, the president's designated leader of the welfare reform reauthorization effort, is a long-established fathers' rights advocate must be tempered with input from those of us who have lived in the "system" because our husbands have walked out on us. If welfare reform is really going to work, it must be premised on facts, not stereotypes. President Bush's plan for reauthorization includes the allocation of millions of dollars for fatherhood initiatives. Millions of dollars that would be better spent going to the children that have been abandoned instead of to the men that have abandoned them.

Throwing money at fathers who walk away from vulnerable and needy children will not morph them into responsible fathers. President Bush, Dr. Horn, and the rest of the administration cannot legislate responsibility. They cannot change the hearts of men who care more about making their car payment than feeding their child.

It is past time for President Bush, Dr. Horn, and all legislators in a position of government authority to listen to "The Other Side of Welfare." It is not all about unwed teenagers and lazy, bon-bon eating moms with twelve children. Welfare is about children and families who are financially and morally neglected by an absent parent—unfortunately, and usually, a husband and father. Until the administration, media, and public at large understand that a majority of mothers and children needing public assistance do so only because, and after, a husband and father has deserted them, there will be no true welfare reform. Relevant statistics and symptoms might change. The underlying problem will remain.

The United States must not tolerate parents who leave their children without sufficient support to meet their most basic needs. In our country of immense prosperity, it must become socially and culturally unacceptable to desert a family if there is to be any viable hope of reversing the ever-increasing trend of fathers moving on to new women, new children, new families, and new commitments, while leaving all their previous and existing obligations behind.

At the writing of this epilogue, I sit stuck in an all too familiar dilemma with regard to collecting my children's court-ordered child support. We have not received a penny of support since October 31, 2000, the very date I received my first legal aid paycheck. Eric owes our family more than twenty-five thousand dollars. Although I filed a petition with the court to have a hearing on the arrearage, Eric, as usual, successfully avoided service of the summons. Thus, no hearing occurred. Subsequent to his avoiding service, he moved to a one-bedroom apartment.

Although I have a phone number for him, he refuses to give me an address. So, I will have to subpoena his employer to get his address and begin the process all over again. As a practical matter, if I do get Eric served and bring him before a judge, two things could likely result. One, he could be incarcerated for up to one year for his failure to pay support. If he is locked up, he, of course, will not be able to pay anything. Or, two, because he has reduced his income substantially, the court might reduce the support order. Either way, going to court over the issue will not "fix" the overall problem.

Because of Eric's failure to provide our support, I had to leave my job at Legal Services and take work at a private domestic relations law firm. It ripped my heart to have to leave legal aid, I absolutely loved that work. It was a privilege to be able to help other people who found themselves lost in the same myriad legal frustrations I had found myself in several years ago. The relief that I was able to provide to some mothers and their children was priceless . . . not only to them, but to me as well.

But, when my oldest son came to me to say that I didn't keep enough food in the house, when my paychecks didn't stretch far enough to purchase more food, my heart ripped even more. Because I had chosen their father, and because of my ongoing hope that he would "change," my children were stuck in an all too familiar dilemma . . . having to live with less because of a dad who just doesn't, or won't, care enough to provide for them.

I now work for the Law Office of Betty A. Thompson, in northern Virginia. Miss Thompson has been practicing family law for more than fifty years. She is a living legal legend . . . considered the "best of the best" in her field. I have a lot to learn, and, under her direction, I am certain that I will. I am also certain that I will always long to help other single parents, moms especially.

After a successful hearing, my clients would often give me a hug. Although a hug won't feed my kids, the appreciation and thanks a hug can represent might be more valuable than any retainer fee or billable hour. The law should be about helping and protecting people, especially the most vulnerable. My ultimate goal is to sit as a judge in the Juvenile and Domestic Relations Court of Fairfax County, Virginia, and, one day, perhaps, to run for a state or national political office. As a judge, I would have an enormous opportunity to impact children and families struggling to survive the fallout of family disintegration. As a legislator, I would have an opportunity to draft and propose laws that could be beneficial to and in the best interests of, those same children and families.

A short time after I started working with Miss Thompson, my oldest daughter, April, was scheduled to accompany me to work in order to complete a requirement for her eight-grade civics class. I was supposed to conduct a court tour in the morning for a local junior high school and then proceed to my office in the afternoon to work on my case assignments. The evening before, much to my frustration, my youngest son, Thomas, informed me that he had been suspended from school for the following day, because he had stuck his tongue out at a fellow classmate at his school.

I was obligated to handle the court tour for the junior high school. I had to show up at the office, I had only been at my new job for two weeks. It wouldn't look good to call in "sick" because of a child care dilemma. I needed a quick solution, so I asked April to forgo her day of shadowing me at work and stay home with Thomas. I offered to pay her a fair rate for baby-sitting and suggested that she write her civics essay about being a working single parent and what happens when a child does not or cannot attend school on a particular day.

Child care dilemmas are huge, practical problems for single parents. Child care for sick children is seldom available, and if it is, it is generally prohibitively expensive. And, if my child is ill, I am of the strong conviction that I should be taking care of him or her. What child wants to be left by his or her only reliable parent when feeling sick? Certainly, not any of mine. On that day, April learned a real life lesson about parenthood and responsibility. I am hopeful that such lessons will counter the terrible example she has seen in her dad and will reinforce her desire to find a reliable, responsible, and committed man to marry. I anxiously anticipate the return of April's graded essay. I can't wait to read her teacher's comments about her experience as a single working mom.

In the past, the process of welfare reform reauthorization has been the same tired tune. Stereotypically thinking political leaders jump on board with legislative proposals that are no more grounded in fact than junk mail solicitations for big dollar sweepstakes. Legislators offer the "same old, same old," when they debate the welfare issue. Talk of "able-bodied" recipients working "forty hours per week" instead of living "on the dole" permeates the nightly news and saturates television news magazines.

"Real life" recipients like me are left out of the formal debate, because we "buck" the political assumptions on which many of these leaders bank their policies. Large chunks of federal money are directed toward "fatherhood" programs that accomplish little more than reinforcing and undergirding the "victim" attitude that most delinquent, noncustodial parents thrive on. The ultimate result is the continuing disintegration of the American family, the continuing accrual of child support arrearages across the country, and the continuing trend of fathers walking away from their children and families . . . never to look, or pay, back again. Something has to change!

Appendix 1

Practical Tips for Single Parents

1. If you have any reason to believe that you might find yourself in the position of being or becoming a single parent, be certain to obtain and document the following information regarding the other parent of your child or children:

   a. His or her full, legal name;
   b. His or her social security number;
   c. His or her employment address and telephone number;
   d. His or her health insurance information;
   e. The address of his or her closest relative;
   f. His or her birth date;
   g. His or her current or most recent residence address;
   h. His or her driver's license state of issue and number; and
   i. His or her automobile tag number.

2. Be certain to obtain and keep in an accessible but safe place, your child or children's original, certified birth certificates.
3. Be certain to obtain and keep in an accessible but safe place, your child or children's original social security cards.
4. Know and keep handy the address and telephone number of your local magistrate.
5. Know and keep handy the address and telephone number of your local juvenile and domestic relations court.
6. Know and keep handy the address and telephone number of your local child support enforcement agency.
7. Know and keep handy the address and telephone number of your local department of social services.

8. Know and keep handy the address and telephone number of any health insurance policy and/or company you may use.

9. Visit your local law library and become familiar with the statutes governing family law in your particular state and locality.

10. When being your own advocate, remember to be as objective as possible.

11. When representing yourself in court, remember to be as objective as possible.

12. Provide a certified copy of any court-ordered custody arrangement to the administrative office of your child or children's day care center, provider, or school.

13. Keep a copy of every court order obtained regarding either custody and/or child support in a safe, secure place.

14. Keep a copy of any current custody order with you at all times, perhaps in a purse, wallet, or handbag.

15. Obtain individual counseling for yourself if you are struggling with the demands of being a single parent; not only will it be of benefit to you, it will be of benefit to your children.

16. Seek out other single parents or single parent organizations for support and encouragement.

17. Be honest with your children with regard to the behaviors of their other parent, while being careful to neither degrade nor denigrate that parent.

18. When exchanging the children for visitation, try to be as pleasant as possible.

19. Do not let the stress you might feel as a single parent be exhibited in front of your child or children during visitation exchanges.

20. Attempt to keep the other parent informed regarding your child or children's medical and school records.

21. Do not be afraid to seek out community resources available to you and your child or children.

22. Take time to be involved in activities that are separate from your role as a parent when reasonably possible.

23. Attempt to foster a good relationship for your child or children with their other parent.

24. Be frugal with your finances, but do not place your financial worries on the shoulders of your child and or children. And,

25. Love your child or children as much as you can, every day. Draw from your child or children the motivation that you need to persevere and build a better life for all of you.

ENJOY YOUR CHILDREN—NO MATTER WHAT,
BEFORE LONG, THEY'LL BE GROWN AND GONE.

Appendix 2

Letter from President George Bush Sr.

THE WHITE HOUSE

WASHINGTON

April 21, 1992

Dear Ms. Cave:

Thanks so much for writing and for asking about my agenda for our Nation's future. I appreciate your determination to get the "straight scoop" so that you can make informed decisions as a voter.

While signs point to an economic recovery ahead -- interest rates and inflation are down, housing starts are up, and exports are at record highs -- spurring economic growth and creating jobs remain my top priorities. In January when I addressed the Congress on the State of the Union, I submitted a short-term plan to speed our recovery and a long-term plan to sustain growth and create jobs. This comprehensive set of proposals includes, among other things, tax credits for first-time homebuyers, a $500 increase in the personal tax exemption for children, and a cut in the capital gains tax rate. (By the way, contrary to my opponents' claims that a capital gains cut would "only help the rich," studies have shown that close to two-thirds of those who would benefit from the reduction are taxpayers with annual incomes of less than $50,000: for example, retirees who want to sell their homes but can't afford to lose a large portion of the sale price in order to pay capital gains taxes.)

Instead of passing my short-term initiatives by March 20 as I had asked, the Democrat-controlled Congress sent me a bill that would raise taxes. Because I will not sign legislation that harms the economy and because I believe that government is

2

already too big and spends too much, I vetoed the bill and announced steps that I am taking on my own in order to help the economy. I also renewed my call on Congress to pass the seven-point plan that I submitted earlier and to stop holding the American economy hostage in a partisan game.

The challenges of raising a family today are, of course, not only economic. But as you well know, parents worry about the future of education and health care and about the impact of drugs and crime on the lives of their children. For the sake of America's future, we must put families first. Because so many of our Nation's most pressing social problems are linked to a breakdown in traditional family life and values, I have established a special commission on urban families that will work to identify ways that government can assist families and encourage them to stay together. The Administration is already working to reform welfare programs so that they foster responsibility and self-sufficiency, not a continuing cycle of dependency, and -- you may be especially interested to know -- we are also committed to tracking down deadbeat dads, the ones who ignore their legal and moral obligation to pay child support.

During the months ahead, I will continue to urge Congress to pass the Administration's Comprehensive Violent Crime Control Act, which will help to make our streets and neighborhoods safer. I will also continue to press Congress for action on our AMERICA 2000 Excellence in Education Act, which will give choice to parents and promote excellence in our schools through greater competition and accountability. Finally, I will continue to work for health care reform that is responsible and market-oriented, that will preserve quality and choice, and that will make health care more accessible and more affordable for all Americans. (I am determined to avoid the kind of socialized medicine that would only lead to long lines, waiting lists, and an excessive burden on American taxpayers).

Obviously, this is a very broad view of my agenda for our country's future, Ms. Cave, and I hope that my comments have been helpful. I admire your resolve to speak out and to vote responsibly, in a thoughtful and

3

informed manner. I also applaud your determined efforts to do your best for your children. Rest assured that, on this end, I will continue to make the tough choices and to promote the commonsense policies and programs that are right for America.

Best wishes.

Sincerely,

George Bush

Ms. Pamela Cave
15215 Bannon Hill Court
Chantilly, Virginia 22021

P.S. I am very pleased that you are involved and reaching out to help others. We've been through a very rough time in terms of our economy, but it is improving now, and really so. With this improvement will come economic growth and then, following on, more jobs.

Though I've tried to answer your questions it is so hard to touch on all the issues. I hope your 4 kids are doing fine. Thanks for writing and Good luck — George Bush

Appendix 3

Resource Guide

General

The United States Department of Health and Human Services
1-877-696-6775
200 Independence Avenue, SW
Washington, DC, 20201

The Social Security Administration
1-800-772-1213
6401 Security Blvd.
Baltimore, MD 21235-0001

The Administration for Children and Families
370 L'Enfant Promenade, SW
Washington, DC, 20447

Child Care Aware
1-800-424-2246

Childhelp's National Child Abuse Hotline
1-800-422-4453

National Domestic Violence Hotline
1-800-799-7233
TDD 1-800-787-3224

State Child Support Enforcement Offices

Alabama

Department of Human Resources
Division of Child Support
50 Ripley Street
Montgomery, AL 36130-1801
(334) 242-9300
FAX: (334) 242-0606
1-800-284-4347 [1]

Alaska

Child Support Enforcement Division
550 West 7th Avenue, Suite 310
Anchorage, AK 99501-6699
(907) 269-6900
FAX: (907) 269-6813
1-800-478-3300 [1]

Arizona

Division of Child Support Enforcement
P.O. Box 40458
Phoenix, AZ 85067
(602) 252-4045
(no toll-free number)

Arkansas

Office of Child Support Enforcement
P.O. Box 8133
Little Rock, AR 72203
Street Address: 712 West Third
Little Rock, AR 72201
(501) 682-8398
FAX: (501) 682-6002
1-800-264-2445 [2] (Payments)
1-800-247-4549 [2] (Program)

California

California Department of Child Support Services
Customer and Community Services Branch
P.O. Box 419064, MS-30
Rancho Cordova, CA 95741-9064
FAX: (916) 464-5065
1-866-249-0773

Colorado

Division of Child Support Enforcement
Division of Human Services
303 E. 17th Avenue, Suite 200
Denver, CO 80203-1241
(720) 947-5000
FAX: (720) 947-5006
(no toll-free number)

Connecticut

Department of Social Services
Bureau of Child Support Enforcement
25 Sigourney Street
Hartford, CT 06105-5033
(860) 424-5251
FAX: (860) 951-2996 1-800-228-5437 [2] (problems)
1-800-647-8872 [2] (information)
1-800-698-0572 [2] (payments)

Delaware

Division of Child Support Enforcement
Delaware Health and Social Services
1901 North Dupont Hwy
P.O. Box 904
New Castle, DE 19720
(302) 577-4863, 577-4800
FAX: (302) 577-4873
1-800-464-4357

District of Columbia

Office of Paternity and Child Support Enforcement
Department of Human Services
800 9th Street, S.W., 2nd Floor
Washington, DC 20024-2480
(202) 724-1444
(no toll-free number)

Florida

Child Support Enforcement Program
Department of Revenue
P.O. Box 8030
Tallahassee, FL 32314-8030
(850) 922-9590
FAX: (850) 488-4401
(no toll-free number)

Georgia

Child Support Enforcement
P.O. Box 38450
Atlanta, GA 30334-0450
(404) 657-3851
FAX: (404) 657-3851
1-800-227-7993 [1] (for 706 and 912 area codes)
(from area codes 404 and 770, dial code + 657-2780)

Guam

Department of Law
Child Support Enforcement Office
238 Archbishop F. C. Flores, 7th Floor
Agana, GU 96910
011 (671) 475-3360
(no toll-free number)

Hawaii

Child Support Enforcement Agency
Department of Attorney General
Kakuhihewa State Office Building
601 Kamokila Boulevard, Suite 251
Kapolei, HI 96707
(808) 587-3695
(808) 692-7134
(no toll-free number)

Idaho

Bureau of Child Support Services
Department of Health and Welfare
P.O. Box 83720
Boise, ID 83720-0036
(208) 334-6535
FAX: (208) 334-0666
1-800-356-9868 [2]

Illinois

Illinois Department of Public Aid
Division of Child Support Enforcement
Marriott Building
509 South Sixth Street
Springfield, IL 62701-1825
(217) 524-4602
FAX: (217) 524-4608
1-800-447-4278 [1]

Indiana

Child Support Bureau
402 West Washington Street, Rm W360
Indianapolis, IN 46204
(317) 233-5437
FAX: (317) 233-4932 [2]
1-800-840-8757

Iowa

Bureau of Collections
Department of Human Services
Hoover Building - 5th Floor
Des Moines, IA 50319
(515) 242-5530
FAX: (515) 281-8854
1-888-229-9223

Kansas

Child Support Enforcement Program
Department of Social and Rehabilitation Services
P.O. Box 497
Topeka, KS 66601
Street Address:
300 S.W. Oakley Street
Biddle Building
Topeka, KS 66606
(785) 296-3237
FAX: (913) 296-5206 1-800-432-0152 [2] (Withholding)
1-800-570-6743 [2] (collections)
1-800-432-3913 [2] (fraud hotline)

Kentucky

Division of Child Support Enforcement Cabinet for Human Resources
P.O. Box 2150
Frankfort, KY 40602
(502) 564-2285
FAX: (502) 564-5988
1-800-248-1163 [2]

Louisiana

Support Enforcement Services
Office of Family Support
P.O. Box 94065

Baton Rouge, LA 70804-4065
(225) 342-4780
FAX: (504) 342-7397
1-800-256-4650 [1] (Payments)

Maine

Division of Support Enforcement and Recovery
Bureau of Income Maintenance
Department of Human Services
State House Station
11 Whitten Road
Augusta, ME 04333
(207) 287-2886
FAX: (207) 287-5096
1-800-371-3101 [1]

Maryland

Child Support Enforcement
Administration
Department of Human Resources
311 West Saratoga Street
Baltimore, MD 21201
(410) 767-7619
FAX: (410) 333-8992
1-800-234-1528 [2]

Massachusetts

Child Support Enforcement Division
Department of Revenue
141 Portland Street
Cambridge, MA 02139-1937
(617) 577-7200
FAX: (617) 621-4991
1-800-332-2733 [2]

MICHIGAN

Office of Child Support
Family Independence Agency
P.O. Box 30478
Lansing, MI 48909-7978
(517) 373-7570
FAX: (517) 373-4980
(no toll-free number)

MINNESOTA

Office of Child Support Enforcement
Department of Human Services
444 Lafayette Road, 4th floor
St. Paul, MN 55155-3846
(651) 296-2542
FAX: (651) 297-4450
(no toll-free number)

MISSISSIPPI

Division of Child Support Enforcement
Department of Human Services
P.O. Box 352
Jackson, MS 39205
(601) 359-4861
FAX: (601) 359-4415
1-800-434-5437 (Jackson) [2]
1-800-354-6039 (Hines, Rankin and Madison Counties

MISSOURI

Department of Social Services
Division of Child Support Enforcement
P.O. Box 2320
Jefferson City, MO 65102-2320
(573) 751-4301
FAX: (573) 751-8450
1-800-859-7999 [2]

MONTANA

Child Support Enforcement Division
Department of Public Health and Human Services
P.O. Box 202943
Helena, MT 59620
(406) 442-7278
FAX: (406) 444-1370
1-800-346-5437 [1]

NEBRASKA

Nebraska Department of Health and Human Services
Child Support Enforcement Office
P.O. Box 94728
Lincoln, NE 68509-4728
(402) 479-5555
FAX: (402) 471-9455
1-800-831-4573 [1]

NEVADA

Child Support Enforcement Program
Nevada State Welfare Division
2527 North Carson Street
Carson City, NV 89710
(775) 687-4744
FAX: (702) 684-8026
1-800-992-0900 x 4744 [1]

NEW HAMPSHIRE

Office of Child Support
Division of Human Services
Health and Human Services Building
6 Hazen Drive
Concord, NH 03301-6531
(603) 271-4427
FAX: (603) 271-4787
1-800-852-3345 x 4427 [1]

New Jersey

Division of Family Development
Department of Human Services
Bureau of Child Support and Paternity Programs CN 716
Trenton, NJ 08625-0716
(609) 588-2915
FAX: (609) 588-2354
1-800-621-5437 [2]

New Mexico

Child Support Enforcement Bureau
Department of Human Services
P.O. Box 25109
Santa Fe, NM 87504
Street Address:
2025 S. Pacheco
Santa Fe, NM 87504
(505) 476-7040
FAX: (505) 827-7285
1-800-288-7207 [1]
1-800-585-7631

New York

Office of Child Support Enforcement
Department of Social Services
P.O. Box 14
Albany, NY 12260
Street Address:
One Commerce Plaza
Albany, NY 12260
(518) 474-9081
FAX: (518) 486-3127
1-800-342-3009

North Carolina

Child Support Enforcement Section
Division of Social Services
Department of Human Resources
100 East Six Forks Road
Raleigh, NC 27609-7750
(919) 571-4114
FAX: (919) 571-4126
1-800-992-9457 [1]

North Dakota

Department of Human Services
Child Support Enforcement Agency
P.O. Box 7190
Bismarck, ND 58507-7190
(701) 328-3582
FAX: (701) 328-5497
1-800-755-8530 [1]

Ohio

Office of Child Support Enforcement
Department of Human Services
30 East Broad Street - 31st Floor
Columbus, OH 43266-0423
(614) 752-6561
FAX: (614) 752-9760
1-800-686-1556 [1]

Oklahoma

Department of Human Services
P.O. Box 53552
Oklahoma City, OK 73125
Street Address:
2409 N. Kelley Avenue
Annex Building
Oklahoma City, OK 73111

(405) 522-5871
FAX: (405) 522-2753
1-800-522-2922 [2]

Oregon

Department of Justice
Division of Child Support
1495 Edgewater N.W., Suite 290
Salem, OR 97304
(503) 986-5950
FAX: (503) 391-5526
1-800-850-0228 [1]
1-800-850-0294 [1] Rotary

Pennsylvania

Bureau of Child Support Enforcement
Department of Public Welfare
P.O. Box 8018
Harrisburg, PA 17105
(717) 783-5184
FAX: (717) 787-9706
1-800-932-0211 [2]

Puerto Rico

Child Support Enforcement
Department of Social Services
P.O. Box 3349
San Juan, PR 00902-9938
Street Address:
Majagua Street, Bldg. 2
Wing 4, 2nd Floor
Miramar, PR 00902-9938
(787) 767-1500
FAX: (787) 723-6187
(no toll-free number)

Rhode Island

Rhode Island Child Support Services
Department of Human Services
77 Dorrance Street
Providence, RI 02903
(401) 222-2847
FAX: (401) 277-6674
1-800-638-5437 [1]

South Carolina

Department of Social Services
Child Support Enforcement Division
P.O. Box 1469
Columbia, SC 29202-1469
(803) 898-9341
FAX: (803) 737-6032
1-800-768-5858 [2]
1-800-768-6779 [1] (Payments)

South Dakota

Office of Child Support Enforcement
Department of Social Services
700 Governor's Drive
Pierre, SD 57501
(605) 773-3641
FAX: (605) 773-5246
(no toll-free number)

Tennessee

Child Support Services
Department of Human Services
Citizens Plaza Building - 12th Floor
400 Deadrick Street
Nashville, TN 37248-7400
(615) 313-4880
FAX: (615) 532-2791
1-800-838-6911 [2]

TEXAS

Office of the Attorney General
State Office
Child Support Division
P.O. Box 12017
Austin, TX 78711-2017
(512) 460-6000
FAX: (512) 834-9712
1-800-252-8014 [2]

UTAH

Bureau of Child Support Services
Department of Human Services
P.O. Box 45011
Salt Lake City, UT 84145-0011
(801) 536-8500
FAX: (801) 536-8509
1-800-257-9156 [2]

VERMONT

Office of Child Support
103 South Main Street
Waterbury, VT 05671-1901
(802) 241-2313
FAX: (802) 244-1483
1-800-786-3214 [2]

VIRGIN ISLANDS

Paternity and Child Support Division
Department of Justice
GERS Building, 2nd Floor
48B-50C Krondprans Gade
St. Thomas, VI 00802
(340) 775-3070
FAX: (809) 774-9710
(no toll-free number)

Virginia

Division of Support Enforcement
Department of Social Services
730 East Broad Street
Richmond, VA 23219
(804) 692-1428
FAX: (804) 692-1405
1-800-468-8894 [1]

Washington

Division of Child Support
Department of Social and Health Services
P.O. Box 9162
Olympia, WA 98507-9162
Street address:
712 Pear Street, S.E.
Olympia, WA 98507
(360) 664-5000
FAX: (206) 586-3274
1-800-922-4306 [2]

West Virginia

Child Support Enforcement Division
Department of Health and Human Resources
1900 Kanawha Boulevard East
Capitol Complex, Building 6, Room 817
Charleston, WV 25305
(304) 558-3780
1-800-249-3778 [2]

Wisconsin

Division of Economic Support
P.O. Box 7935
Madison, WI 53707-7935
Street Address:
1 West Wilson Street

Room 382
Madison, WI 53707
(608) 266-9909
FAX: (608) 267-2824
(no toll-free number)

WYOMING

Child Support Enforcement
Department of Family Services
Hathaway Building
2300 Capital Avenue, 3rd Floor
Cheyenne, WY 82002-0490
(307) 777-6948
FAX: (307) 777-3693
1-800-457-3659 [2]

State Human Services Administrators

Mr. Bill Fuller
Commissioner
Alabama State Department of Human Resources
50 Ripley Street
Montgomery, AL 36130-4000
Phone: (334) 242-1160
FAX: (334) 242-0198

Mr. Jay Lively
Commissioner
Alaska Department of Health and Social Services
P.O. Box 110601
Juneau, AK 99811-0601
Phone: (907) 465-3030
FAX: (907) 465-3068

Dr. Uiagalelie Leaofi
Director
American Samoa Department of Human and Social Services
P.O. Box 997534
Pago Pago, AS 96799
Phone: 011 (684) 633-2969
FAX: 011 (684) 633-7449

Mr. John L. Clayton
Director
Arizona Department of Economic Security
P.O. Box 6123, Site Code 010A
Phoenix, AZ 85005
Phone: (602) 542-5678
FAX: (602) 542-5339

Mr. Kurt Knickrehm
Director
Arkansas Department of Human Services
329 Donaghey Plaza South
Seventh and Main Streets
P.O. Box 1437

Little Rock, AR 72203-1437
Phone: (501) 682-8650
FAX: (501) 682-6836

Mr. Grantland Johnson
Secretary
California Health and Human Services Agency
1600 Ninth Street, Room 460
Sacramento, CA 95814
Phone: (916) 654-3345
FAX: (916) 654-3343

Ms. Rita Saenz
Director
California Department of Social Services
744 P Street
Mail Stop 17-11
Sacramento, CA 95814
Phone: (916) 657-2598
FAX: (916) 653-1695

Mrs. Marva Livingston Hammons
Executive Director
Colorado Department of Human Services
1575 Sherman Street, 8th floor
Denver, CO 80203-1714
Phone: (303) 866-5096
FAX: (303) 866-4740

Ms. Patricia A. Wilson-Coker
Commissioner
Connecticut Department of Social Services
25 Sigourney Street
Hartford, CT 06106-2055
Phone: (860) 424-5008
FAX: (860) 424-5129

Mr. Vincent P. Meconi
Secretary
Delaware Health and Social Services
Herman M. Holloway Sr., Campus

Main Administration Building, 1st floor
1901 N. DuPont Highway
New Castle, DE 19720
Phone: (302) 577-4502
FAX: (302) 577-4510

Ms. Carolyn W. Colvin
Director
District of Columbia Department of Human Services
801 East Building
2700 Martin Luther King Jr. Ave., SE
Washington, DC 20032-0247
Phone: (202) 279-6016
FAX: (202) 279-6014

Judge Kathleen Kearney
Secretary
Florida Department of Children and Families
Building 1, Room 202
1317 Winewood Boulevard
Tallahassee, FL 32399-0700
Phone: (850) 487-1111
FAX: (850) 922-2993

Mr. Ruben J. King-Shaw
Director
Florida Agency for Health Care
Administration
Fort Knox Building 3
2727 Mahan Drive
Suite 3116
Tallahassee, FL 32308
Phone: (850) 922-3809
FAX: (850) 488-0043

Ms. Juanita Blout-Clark
Director
Georgia Department of Human Resources
Division of Family and Children Services
2 Peachtree Street

Atlanta, GA 30303
Phone: (404) 657-7660
FAX: (404) 657-5105

Mr. Jim Martin
Commissioner
Georgia Department of Human Resources
2 Peach Tree Street, NW, Suite 29-250
Atlanta, GA 30303
Phone: (404) 656-5680
FAX: (404) 651-8669

Mr. Dennis G. Rodriguez
Director
Guam Department of Public Health and Social Services
P.O. Box 2816
Agana, GU 96932
Phone: 011 (671) 734-7102
FAX: 011 (671) 734-5910

Ms. Susan Chandler
Director
Hawaii Department of Human Services
P.O. Box 339
1390 Miller Street, Room 209
Honolulu, HI 96813
Phone: (808) 586-4997
FAX: (808) 586-4890

Mr. Karl B. Kurtz
Director
Idaho Department of Health and Welfare
P.O. Box 83720
450 West State Street, 10th Floor
Boise, ID 83720-0036
Phone: (208) 334-5500
FAX: (208) 334-6558

Ms. Linda Renee Baker
Secretary
Illinois Department of Human Services

Harris Building, 3rd floor
210 South Grand Avenue, East
Springfield, IL 62762
Phone: (217) 557-1601
FAX: (217) 557-1647

Mr. John Jay Boyce
Director
Division of Family and Children
Indiana Family and Social Services Administration
W392 Government Center South
402 West Washington Street
P.O. Box 7083
Indianapolis, IN 46207-7083
Phone: (317) 232-4705
FAX: (317) 232-4490

Mr. John Hamilton
Secretary
Indiana Family and Social Services Administration
402 West Washington Street
Room W-461
Indianapolis, IN 46204
Phone: (317) 233-4690
FAX: (317) 233-4693

Ms. Jessie Rasmussen
Director
Iowa Department of Human Services
East 13th Street and Walnut
Hoover State Office Building
Des Moines, IA 50319-0114
Phone: (515) 281-5452
FAX: (515) 281-4597

Ms. Janet Schalansky
Secretary
Kansas Department of Social and Rehabilitation Services
Docking State Office Building, 6th Floor
915 SW Harrison

Topeka, KS 66612-1570
Phone: (913) 296-3271
FAX: (913) 296-4685

Ms. Viola P. Miller
Secretary
Kentucky Cabinet for Families and Children
275 East Main Street, 4th floor West
Frankfort, KY 40621
Phone: (502) 564-7130
FAX: (502) 564-3866

Ms. J. Renea Austin-Duffin
Secretary
Louisiana Department of Social Services
P.O. Box 3776
755 N. 3rd Street, RM 201
Baton Rouge, LA 70821
Phone: (225) 342-0286
FAX: (225) 342-8636

Mr. Kevin W. Concannon
Commissioner
Maine Department of Human Services
11 State House Station
221 State Street
Augusta, ME 04333
Phone: (207) 287-2736
FAX: (207) 287-3005

Ms. Emelda P. Johnson
Secretary
Maryland Department of Human Resources
Saratoga State Center
311 West Saratoga Street
10th Floor
Baltimore, MD 21201
Phone: (410) 767-7109
FAX: (410) 333-0099

Ms. Claire McIntire
Commissioner
Massachusetts Department of Transitional Assistance
600 Washington Street
Boston, MA 02111
Phone: (617) 348-8410
FAX: (617) 348-8575

Mr. James K. Haveman
Director
Michigan Department of Community Health
Lewis Cass Building
320 South Walnut Street
Lansing, MI 48913
Phone: (517) 335-0267
FAX: (517) 373-4288

Mr. Douglas Howard
Director
Michigan Family Independence Agency
235 South Grand Avenue
Lansing, MI 48909
Phone: (517) 373-2000
FAX: (517) 335-6101

Mr. Michael O'Keefe
Commissioner
Minnesota Department of Human Services
444 Lafayette Road
St. Paul, MN 55155-3815
Phone: (651) 296-2701
FAX: (651) 296-5868

Ms. Janice Broome Brooks
Executive Director
Mississippi Department of Human Services
750 North State Street
Jackson, MS 39202
Phone: (601) 359-4480
FAX: (601) 359-4477

Mr. Steve Renne
Director
Missouri Department of Social Services
Broadway State Office Building
221 W. High Street
Jefferson City, MO 65102
Phone: (573) 751-4815
FAX: (573) 751-3203

Ms. Gail Gray
Director
Montana Department of Public Health and Human Services
111 North Sanders
P.O. Box 4210
Helena, MT 59604-4210
Phone: (406) 444-5622
FAX: (406) 444-1970

Mr. Hank G. Hudson
Administrator
Human and Community Services Division
Montana Department of Public Health and Human Services
P.O. Box 202952
Helena, MT 59620-2952
Phone: (406) 444-5901
FAX: (406) 444-2547

Mr. Steve Curtiss
Director
Nebraska Department of Health and Human Services
Finance and Support
301 Centennial Mall South
P.O. Box 95026
Lincoln, NE 68509-5026
Phone: (402) 471-8553
FAX: (402) 471-9449

Mr. Ron Ross
Director
Nebraska Department of Health and Human Services

P.O. Box 59604
Lincoln, NE 68509-5044
Phone: (402) 471-9106
FAX: (402) 471-0820

Mr. Michael J. Willden
Director
Nevada Department of Human Resources
505 East King Street, Suite 600
Carson City, NV 89710
Phone: (775) 687-4730
FAX: (775) 687-4733

Mr. Richard A. Chevrefils
Assistant Commissioner
Office of Family Services
New Hampshire Department of Health and Human Services
129 Pleasant Street
Concord, NH 033011-6505
Phone: (603) 271-4321
FAX: (603) 271-4727

Mr. Donald L. Shumway
Commissioner
New Hampshire Department of Health and Human Services
State Office Park South
129 Pleasant St., Brown Bldg.
Concord, NH 03301-3857
Phone: (603) 271-4331
FAX: (603) 271-4232

Mr. James W. Smith Jr.
Acting Commissioner
New Jersey Department of Human Services
P.O. Box 700
Trenton, NJ 08625-0700
Phone: (609) 292-3717
FAX: (609) 292-3824

Ms. Robin Dozier Otten
Deputy Secretary
New Mexico Human Services Department
P.O. Box 2348
2009 South Pacheco
Santa Fe, NM 87504-2348
Phone: (505) 827-7750
FAX: (505) 827-6286

Mr. John A. Johnson
Commissioner
New York State Office of Children and Family Services
52 Washington Street
Rensselaer, NY 12144
Phone: (518) 473-8437
FAX: (518) 473-9131

Mr. Brian Wing
Commissioner
New York State Department of Family Assistance
Office of Temporary and Disability Assistance
40 North Pearl Street
Albany, NY 12243
Phone: (518) 474-9475/4152
FAX: (518) 486-6255

Ms. Carmen Hooker Buell
Secretary
North Carolina Department of Health and Human Services
101 Blair Drive
Raleigh, NC 27603
Phone: (919) 733-4534
FAX: (919) 715-4645

Ms. Carol K. Olson
Executive Director
North Dakota Department of Human Services
State Capitol - Judicial Wing
600 East Boulevard
Bismarck, ND 58505

Phone: (701) 328-2310
FAX: (701) 328-1545

Ms. Sandy Blunt
Assistant Director
Ohio Department of Jobs and Family Service
30 East Broad Street, 32nd Floor
Columbus, OH 43266-0423
Phone: (614) 466-6282
FAX: (614) 466-2815

Mr. Tom Hayes
Director
Ohio Department of Jobs and Family Services
30 East Broad Street, 32nd Floor
Columbus, OH 43266-0423
Phone: (614) 466-6282
FAX: (614) 466-2815

Mr. Howard A. Hendrick
Director
Oklahoma Department of Human Services
P.O. Box 25352
Oklahoma City, OK 73125-0352
Phone: (405) 521-3646
FAX: (405) 521-6458

Mr. Mike Fogarty
Chief Executive Officer
Oklahoma Health Care Authority
4545 North Lincoln Boulevard
Suite 124
Oklahoma City, OK 73105
Phone: (405) 522-7300
FAX: (405) 522-7471

Mr. Bobby Mink
Director
Oregon Department of Human Services
500 Summer Street, N.E.
Salem, OR 97310-1012

Phone: (503) 945-5944
FAX: (503) 378-2897

Ms. Feather O. Houstoun
Secretary
Pennsylvania Department of Public Welfare
P.O. Box 2675
Harrisburg, PA 17105-2675
Phone: (717) 787-2600
FAX: (717) 772-2062

Ms. Angie Varela-Llavona
Secretary
Puerto Rico Department of The Family
P.O. Box 11398
San Juan, PR 00910-1398
Phone: (787) 725-4511
FAX: (787) 723-1223

Ms. Christine Ferguson
Director
Rhode Island Department of Human Services
600 New London Avenue
Cranston, RI 02920
Phone: (401) 462-2121
FAX: (401) 462-3677

Ms. Elizabeth G. Patterson
Director
South Carolina Department of Social Services
1535 Confederate Avenue
P.O. Box 1520
Columbia, SC 29202-1520
Phone: (803) 898-7360
FAX: (803) 898-7276

Mr. James Ellenbecker
Secretary
South Dakota Department of Human Services
700 Governors Drive
Pierre, SD 57501-2291

Phone: (605) 773-3165
FAX: (605) 773-4855

Ms. Natasha Metcalf
Commissioner
Tennessee Department of Human Services
Citizens Plaza Building, 15th Floor
400 Deaderick Street
Nashville, TN 37248-0200
Phone: (615) 313-4700
FAX: (615) 741-4165

Mr. Jim Hine
Commissioner
Texas Department of Human Services
701 West 51st Street
P.O. Box 149030
Mail Code W-619
Austin, TX 78714-9030
Phone: (512) 438-3030
FAX: (512) 438-4220

Ms. Diane D. Rath
Chair and Commissioner Representing the Public
Texas Work Force Commission
101 East 15th Street
Austin, TX 78778
Phone: (512) 463-2800
FAX: (512) 463-1289

Mrs. Robin Arnold-Williams
Executive Director
Utah Department of Human Services
120 North 200 West, Room 319
Salt Lake City, UT 84145-0500
Phone: (801) 538-3998/4001
FAX: (801) 538-4016

Mr. Rod Betit
Executive Director
Utah Department of Health

P.O. Box 141000
2288 North 1460 West
Salt Lake City, UT 84114-1000
Phone: (801) 538-6111
FAX: (801) 538-3606

Mr. Robert C. Gross
Executive Director
Utah Department of Workforce Services
140 E. 300 South
Salt Lake City, UT 84103
Phone: (801) 526-9210
FAX: (801) 526-9211

Ms. Eileen Elliot
Commissioner
Vermont Department of Social Welfare
103 South Main Street
Waterbury, VT 05671-1201
Phone: (802) 241-2853
FAX: (802) 241-2830

Ms. Sedonia Halbert
Acting Commissioner
Virgin Islands Department of Human Services
Knud Hansen Complex Building A
1303 Hospital Grounds
St. Thomas, VI 00802
Phone: (304) 774-0930
FAX: (304) 774-3466

Ms. Sonia Rivero
Commissioner
Virginia Department of Social Services
Theatre Row Building
730 East Broad Street, 9th Floor
Richmond, VA 23219-1849
Phone: (804) 692-1900
FAX: (804) 692-1949

Mr. Louis Rossiter
Secretary
Virginia Health and Human Resources
202 North 9th Street
Suite 622
Richmond, VA 23219
Phone: (804) 786-7765
FAX: (804) 371-6984

Mr. Dennis Braddock
Secretary
Washington Department of Social and Health Services
115 Washington Street, SE
P.O. Box 45010
Olympia, WA 98504-5010
Phone: (360) 902-7800
FAX: (360) 902-7848

Mr. Frederick Boothe
Commissioner
Bureau of Children and Families
West Virginia Department of Health and Human Resources
350 Capitol Street, Room 730
Charleston, WV 25301-3711
Phone: (304) 558-0999
FAX: (304) 558-4194

Mr. Paul L. Nusbaum
Secretary
West Virginia Department of Health and Human Resources
State Capitol Complex Bldg. 3
Room 206
Charleston, WV 25305-0500
Phone: (304) 558-0684
FAX: (304) 558-1130

Ms. Phyllis J. Dubé
Secretary
Wisconsin Department of Health and Family Services
P.O. Box 7850

Madison, WI 53707-7850
Phone: (608) 266-9622
FAX: (608) 266-7882

Ms. Jennifer Reinert
Secretary
Wisconsin Department of Workforce Development
P.O. Box 7946
Madison, WI 53707-7946
Phone: (608) 266-7552

Ms. Susan Lehman
Director
Wyoming Department of Family Services
Hathaway Building
2300 Capitol Avenue
Cheyenne, WY 82002-0490
Phone: (307) 777-7564
FAX: (307) 777-7747

Mr. Garry L. McKee
Director
Wyoming Department of Health
117 Hathaway Building
2300 Capitol Avenue
Cheyenne, WY 82002-0490
Phone: (307) 777-7656
FAX: (307) 777-7439

Bibliography

Association for Children for Enforcement of Support, Inc. *Aces National News.* Spring 2002.

Bane, Mary Jo, and David T. Ellwood. "One-fifth of the Nations' Children: Why Are They Poor?" *Sci.* 245 (1989): 1047.

Carter v. Morrow, 562 F. Supp. 311 (1983).

Conway v. Conway, 395 S. E. 2d 464, 467 (Va. 1990)

Ellwood, David T. *Poor Support: Poverty in the American Family.* 1988.

Ellwood, David T., and Mary Jo Bane. *The Impact of Aid to Families with Dependent Children on Family Structure and Living Arrangements.* 1985.

Legler, Paul K. "The Coming Revolution in Child Support Policy: Implications of the 1996 Welfare Act." *Family Law Quarterly* 30 (1996): 521.

Public Law No. 74-271, Stat. 620 (1935), The Social Security Act of 1935. Codified as amended at 42 United States Code, Sections 501-617, 1935.

Public Law No. 93-378, 98 Stat. 1305 (1984), The Child Support Amendments of 1984.

Public Law No. 93-647, 88 Stat. 2337 (1974), Amendment to the Social Security Act.

Public Law No. 100-485, 102 Stat. 2343 (1988), The Family Support Act of 1988.

Public Law No. 103-66, 107 Stat. 312 (1993), The Omnibus Budget Reconciliation Act of 1993.

Public Law No. 104-193, 110 Stat. 2105 (1996), The Personal Responsibility and Work Opportunity Reconciliation Act (PRWORA).

Roberts, Barbara, J.D., Michael R. Henry, J.D., and Lavon Loynd, J.D. *Effective Enforcement Techniques for Child Support Obligations,* 2d Edition. The U.S. Department of Health and Human Services, Office of Child Support Enforcement, and the National Institute for Child Support Enforcement, 1987.

Smith, Marilyn Ray. *Policy Studies, Inc., Massachusetts Paternity Acknowledgement Program: Implementation, Analysis, and Program Results.* Child Support Enforcement Division for Massachusetts Department of Revenue, 1995.

Sorenson, Elaine, *Noncustodial Fathers: Can They Afford to Pay More Child Support?* The Urban Institute, 1994.

U.S. Bureau of the Census. *Child Support and Alimony Supplement.* Current Population Survey, 1983.

———. *Child Support and Alimony Supplement.* Current Population Survey, 1989.

———. *Child Support for Custodial Mothers and Fathers.* Current Population Reports Series P60-187, 1991.

———. *Family Disruption and Economic Hardship: The Short-Run Picture for Children.* Current Population Reports Series P-70, no. 23, 1991.

———. *Survey of Income and Education.* 1975.

U.S. Department of Health and Human Services. *Report to Congress on Out-of-Wedlock Childbearing.* 1995.

U.S. Department of Health and Human Services, Working Group on Welfare Reform, Family Support, and Independence. *Background Papers on Welfare Reform: Child Support Enforcement* 3, 1994.

U.S. House of Representatives Ways and Means Committee. *Child Support Enforcement and Welfare Reform: Hearings before the Subcommittee on Human Resources,* 104th Cong., 1st sess., 1995. Testimony of David T. Ellwood.

———. *Contract with America—Welfare Reform: Hearings before the Subcommittee on Human Resources,* 104th Cong., 1st sess., 1995. Testimony of Kevin Aslanian of the National Welfare Reform and Rights Union, pp. 1346, 1350.

———. *Contract with America—Welfare Reform: Hearings before the Subcommittee on Human Resources,* 104th Cong., 1st sess., 1995. Testimony of Ronald K. Henry of the Men's Health Network, p. 1289.

———. *Hearing on Child Support and Fatherhood Proposals,* June 28, 2001. Statement of Chairman Wally Herger, the Subcommittee on Human Resources.

———. *Hearing on Child Support and Fatherhood Proposals,* June 28, 2001. Statement of Frank Fuentes, acting deputy commissioner, the Office of Child Support Enforcement Administration for Children and Families.

———. *Hearings before the Subcommittee on Human Resources,* March 15, 2001. Statement of Frank Fuentes, acting deputy commissioner, the Office of Child Support Enforcement Administration for Children and Families.

———. *Hearings before the Subcommittee on Human Resources,* March 15, 2001. Statement of Nathaniel L. Young Jr., director, the Virginia Department of Social Services, Division of Peggy Child Support Enforcement.

———. *Overview of Entitlement Programs,* Table H-27, 1994, p. 1210.

Virginia Code. Section 20–61 (1977), Desertion and Nonsupport.

Washington State Office of Child Support Enforcement, Paternity Acknowledgement Program. *Program Summary.* 1991.

Index

GOSHEN COLLEGE - GOOD LIBRARY
3 9310 01023212 0